WORDS IN CONTEXT

WORDS
IN
CONTEXT

**A Japanese Perspective on
Language and Culture**

TAKAO SUZUKI
Translated by AKIRA MIURA

KODANSHA INTERNATIONAL
Tokyo • New York • London

Originally published in Japanese by Iwanami Shoten, Tokyo, in 1973 under the
title *Kotoba to Bunka*.

Previously published by Kodansha International as *Japanese and the Japanese:
Words in Culture* in 1978. Chapter 5, "Values Which Give Meaning to Facts,"
and a new preface have been added to revised edition.

Distributed in the United States by Kodansha America, Inc., and in the United
Kingdom and continental Europe by Kodansha Europe Ltd.

Published by Kodansha International Ltd., 17–14 Otowa 1-chome, Bunkyo-ku,
Tokyo 112–8652, and Kodansha America, Inc.

ISBN-13: 978–4–7700–2780–1
ISBN-10: 4–7700–2780–X

First edition, 1978
First revised paperback edition, 1984
First trade paperback edition, 2001
15 14 13 12 11 10 09 08 07 06   10 9 8 7 6 5 4 3 2

www.kodansha-intl.com

Contents

NOTES:

Japanese words are romanized according to the modified Hepburn system.

The five simple vowels are pronounced: *a* as in father, *i* as in *see*, *u* as in mood, *e* as in bed and *o* as in comb, and the dipthongs are pronounceable on the basis of their components. Vowel length is contrastive, either very short or of double length. *Ojisan* 'uncle' and *ojisan* 'grandfather,' for example, are differentiated by the length of the second vowel. (The macron indicates the long vowel, but this has not been used in the case of well-known place names, such as Tokyo.)

The vowels are like those in English. However, *g* at the beginning of a word is always hard, and within a word and in the particle *ga*, it is pronounced [ŋ], at least in Tokyo speech. *R* is a flap *r*, sometimes resembling English *t* or *d* more than the retroflex *r*. *N* after a vowel is syllabic and before *b*, *m*, *n* and *p* has a slightly nasal articulation.

Syllable by syllable pronunciation on the basis of the romanization is acceptable (*bu-n-ka* 'culture'), though vowels, particularly *u*, are sometimes elided (*su-ki-ya-ki—s'ki-ya-ki*).

The grammar of certain sentences cited in this book varies from that usually shown in textbooks of Japanese. This is because the sentences represent the actual spoken language, rather than the written language or model sentences.

An asterisk at the beginning of a sentence is in accordance with the conventional method in linguistics of indicating that a sentence, while it may be inferred by analogy with other sentences, does not in fact occur in the language, i.e., no examples can be found in either writing or speech.

Preface

The word *bunka* 'culture' has various meanings and uses. Most people probably associate this word with arts like literature, music, and painting. There may also be some who think of culture as something highly refined, basing their image of culture on expressions such as *bunka-kokka*, (lit., 'cultured nation'), *bunka-jin*, (lit., 'cultured person'), and *bunkateki na seikatsu*, (lit., 'cultured living').

However, what I call *culture* in this book is a set of behavior and thought patterns that are peculiar to a certain group of people and are passed on from parent to child, from ancestor to descendant. For example, a Japanese indicates himself by pointing to his nose with his forefinger; in contrast, a Westerner usually points to his chest with his thumb. These two ways of indicating oneself reveal a cultural difference. In other words, if we remove all instinctive or inherent elements from the various principles which govern human behavior, the remainder, that is, the part that concerns social restrictions (or customs) and is largely transmittable from generation to generation, is what is called *culture*.

Most linguistic activities fall under this definition of *culture*. Man can only cry at birth, but as he grows, he gradually learns to talk. The language he acquires and the way he speaks it depend entirely on the people around him.

The object of this book is to explain, in the simplest possible terms, in what sense language is culture and how language relates to other aspects of culture.

Interest in language is growing in Japan, and there are a number of excellent books on language, especially technical books or reference books on linguistics. However, non-specialists who are interested in language and would like to learn how it operates, have a hard time finding a suitable introductory book which presents the mystery and fascination of language in such a way that even a casual reader is captivated. I hope that this book will serve as such a guide to the study of language. However, I want to make one point very clear. In my opinion, an introductory book, regardless of its field, cannot and must not be a mere listing of facts. It must present a way of viewing things that is characteristic of the field concerned. Since developing such a view is a dynamic mental activity, the view presented by an introductory book must reflect that of its author. For that reason, I did not hesitate to develop in this book my own view of language, using my own methodology as well as concrete examples. If scholars specializing in linguistics or the study of culture happen to read this book, I would greatly appreciate hearing their comments.

This book is an unabridged English edition of *Kotoba to Bunka* [Language and culture], published in 1973 by Iwanami Shoten, Tokyo. An abridged translation of this book was published by Kodansha International as *Japanese and the Japanese* in 1978. In response to increased demand among English-speaking people for information that gives them insights into the Japanese mentality, the author as well as the publisher decided to publish the book in this new form.

The central theme of the original Japanese edition and that of Chapter 5, which was unfortunately omitted from the previous English edition, deals with the hidden structure underlying the different ways the people of various cultures look at and dissect the world around them.

The author would be gratified if this book could make the reader realize that in today's world, when highly developed systems of communication and transportation have brought the world's nations closer and closer, it is a mistake not to know any foreign language, and infinitely worse to have only a superficial knowledge of a foreign language.

Takao Suzuki
Keio University
Institute of Cultural and Linguistic Studies

1. Language and Culture

Synchronic versus Diachronic

Several years ago in Tokyo, I became acquainted with Mr. T., an American linguist. He had originally started out as a specialist in American Indian languages but had later begun to study Japanese history and dialectology, an interest dating from the postwar days when he was stationed in Japan with the occupation forces. Thus, many years after the war, he was again in Tokyo, this time with his Italian-American wife, an elementary school teacher, and their three daughters.

They rented an old Japanese-style house, where they lived in *tatami* rooms, sitting on *zabuton* (floor cushions). In winter, they kept warm with a *kotatsu* (a foot warmer with a quilt over it) and *kairo* (portable body warmers), and their three daughters attended Japanese schools. Thus the whole family adapted beautifully to Japanese-style living.

One day, as American scholars often do, he invited many friends and acquaintances in his field to his home. After being served cocktails, together with such hors d'oeuvres as Italian-style squid, we were shown into another room for dinner. When everyone was seated, meat and salad were brought in. Interestingly enough, each of us was also served plain white rice in a *donburi*, a large Japanese bowl.

The rice was served in the usual Japanese way, and I knew about the family's living completely in the Japanese style. All these factors must have led me into thinking for a moment that we were supposed to eat the rice as a main course and the meat and salad as side dishes. I picked up the meat dish before me and was ready to pass it to my neighbor, when I sensed that Mrs. T. looked a little puzzled. Suspecting that I was making a blunder, I asked her whether we should eat the rice with the meat or by itself. She answered with a smile that she expected us to finish the rice first. Suddenly it dawned on me that in Italian cuisine rice corresponds to soup, as do macaroni and spaghetti. As a matter of fact, the rice turned out to be a kind of pilaf.

Eating is an important part of a structured entity called culture, and there are rules and restrictions varying from country to country as to what, when, and how to eat, and what not to eat. Everyone knows that Catholics were not supposed to eat meat on Fridays until about a decade ago and that Muslims never eat pork, which they consider unclean. Rules distinctly stating what not to eat are comparatively easy even for foreigners to understand. On the other hand, if an item from one's native cooking appears in a foreign meal but occupies a different position in relation to other items of food in one's own cuisine—i.e., when the value of the same item in a meal as a whole varies from one culture to another—difficult problems arise.

In Japan, white rice may be eaten from the beginning of a meal to the end, but it is considered bad manners to concentrate on eating rice only. One is not observing good manners unless one skips around from nonrice food to rice, from rice to soup, and so on. We might therefore call the relationship between rice and other foods in a Japanese meal concurrent and synchronic: rice may be eaten with soup, pickles, or anything else.

There are, on the other hand, cultures in which one goes through a meal in stages, eating one course at a time. Such a meal may be said to unfold in a distinctively serial, or diachronic, way. Most Occidental countries belong to this group, and Italy is no exception. In Italy, soup and rice are called *minestra* and are eaten before the main meat course begins.

The error I made when I almost ate the meat dish together with the rice was due to the fact that I, finding an item from Japanese cuisine in an Italian meal, tried to give it a Japanese value by assigning it a position according to the structure inherent in my own culture.

I will cite one more nonlinguistic example. The most common form of greeting used when a Japanese meets a friend or an acquaintance is a bow. However, when this same person learns that Occidentals generally shake hands instead of bowing, he starts shaking hands indiscriminately. This is obviously due to his interpretation that a bow and a handshake are acts of equivalent value. Actually, not all occasions when bowing could take place call for handshakes. For example, although in Japan it does not matter which party is the first to bow, in some countries, it is considered bad manners for a man to extend his hand to a woman before she extends her hand. Extending one's hand to anybody one meets might even lead to unnecessary misunderstanding.

Cultural Items and Universal Values

The individual objects and acts that constitute segments of culture are not independent entities nor are they complete by themselves. Each item stands in opposition to many other items in a state of mutual give-and-take; value is thus determined relatively. To equate a certain item (such as a particular kind of food) from one's culture with that discovered in another culture is a mistake because the overall cultural structure is different in most instances.

Most people are totally unaware of the structure of their own culture. Thus they tend to assume that items existing in their culture are in themselves endowed with absolute, and therefore universal, values. This point is essential for the proper understanding of language, which is an important component of culture.

The two examples above demonstrate that when we come into contact with a different culture, especially if our contact is limited, we can rarely grasp the total structure governing individual cultural elements; in most cases, we tend to draw generalizations from that part of the culture which we see or from some untypical examples which we happen to come across. Furthermore, this process of generalization is always based on the structure of our own culture.

This is the crucial point, for when we study a foreign language, we often try to understand it first of all by unconsciously projecting upon it the structure of our own language, in a fashion similar to the above examples. It is only natural that many discrepancies should appear.

The Meaning of *Break*

As a very simple illustration, let us consider the English verb *break*. Japanese junior high school students who first learn the uses of *break* from such sentences as "Who broke the window?" and "He broke his arm" become absolutely convinced that this word must mean the same as the Japanese verbs *waru* and *oru*. Making use of this knowledge in a translantion class, they might confidently translate *Kinō ōkina suika o hōchō de futatsu ni watte (<waru), sore kara yattsu ni kitta* as 'I broke a big watermelon in two with a knife and then divided it into eight pieces.' The teacher would perhaps correct them saying, "You cannot use *broke* here. Use *cut* instead." If they challenged him, saying, "But doesn't *break* mean *waru*, sir?" the teacher might then explain, "It depends. You must realize there's no one-to-one correspondence."

Next, deducing the meaning of *break* from *ude o otta* (<*oru*) 'broke one's arm,' the students might use the word to translate such words as *origami* 'paper-folding art' or *orime* 'a fold; a crease made by folding,' only to be told by the teacher that *fold* is the correct word in this case. They might next learn in a science class that one device that interrupts an electric current is a "circuit breaker." Assuming from this that *break* must also mean *kiru*, the Japanese verb used in that case, they would then start translating the Japanese sentence *Kugi ni yōfuku o hikkakete kitte (<kiru) shimatta* into 'I caught my coat on a nail and broke it,' whereupon the teacher would tell them to use *tore* instead.

Finally losing patience, the students might complain, "But, sir, English makes no sense. It has absolutely no logic," to which the teacher would reply, "Language is not like math; logic doesn't always help. You must study carefully, using your intuition." In the sense that students cannot use their natural inductive or deductive abilities, the brighter they are, the more frustrating they may find foreign-language learning.

Although this illustration may seem exaggerated, the problem is really basic and never ceases to haunt students of foreign languages. But what brings all this about? It is the lack of realization on the teacher's part that meaning and usage in language have structure, and that this structure varies from language to language.

The Structural Nature of Words versus Their Definitions

For the most part, the traditional method of teaching foreign languages has not been concerned with a consideration of the structural framework of language. It has tended to point out so-called equivalents of individual items (i.e., "This word should be translated this way in this particular context"), even though these equivalents may be applicable in only a few instances. The most typical examples of this approach are, unfortunately, found in dictionaries.

If I look up *break* in an English-Japanese dictionary I happen to have handy, I find a list of such Japanese verbs as (1) *kowasu*, (2) *oru*, (3) *yaburu*, (4) *kiru*, etc. Usually, the larger the dictionary, the longer the list, with as many as ten to twenty verbs corresponding in one way or another to *break*. It is no wonder that students become confused.

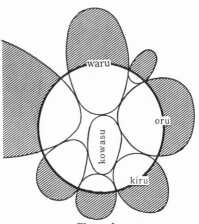

Figure 1

The circle drawn with a heavy line
shows the range of the use of *break*;
all the other circular shapes represent
areas covered by various Japanese
verbs.

Since each of the Japanese words such as *waru* and *oru* corresponds to *break* only in a very limited way, it is not sufficient to give examples of when correspondence occurs. It is
equally necessary to point out when it does not occur.
Otherwise, as in the case of bows and handshakes, we will
not be able to prevent inappropriate generalizations. So far,
however, no dictionary has taken this preventive measure.

If a word from a foreign language is furnished with a
number of Japanese "equivalents," the areas of meaning
where one can confidently use the word will definitely expand. At the same time, however, another ironic result will
be inevitable: the areas where inappropriate generalizations might occur (the dark sections in figure 1) will also

expand rapidly. This difficulty comes from overlooking the following two points. First, within the language to which it belongs, any word stands in close mutual opposition to other words, especially to those close or similar to it in meaning. Their relationship must be understood structurally. Second, even if a given foreign word may be used in the same manner as a particular native word in a certain instance, one must not assume that all the other uses of the former will correspond exactly to those of the latter.

These two points are based on the fact that individual words are structurally different from language to language, which, in turn, corresponds exactly to the point made earlier about a certain dish in cuisines of different cultures: although the dish itself may be the same, it occupies a different position in each case and therefore represents a different value in the meal as a whole.

The idea that language must be studied structurally has been a fundamental one among linguists for the past twenty years or so, although their emphases may vary somewhat. The methods developed by European and Japanese scholars may be summarized as follows: in order to understand the contents of a given word, one must discover and describe the necessary and sufficient conditions that regulate its operations. These linguists have been working more or less in the same direction to develop a method of analyzing and describing the meanings and uses of words, but unfortunately, the results of their research have not contributed much to actual language teaching or dictionary editing.

Comparison of *Nomu* and *Drink*

As an illustration, let me use an example from everyday life. First, let us consider under what conditions the Japanese verb *nomu* 'to drink, to swallow, to smoke, etc.,' may be used. Things that may be the object of an act called *nomu* are first of all fluids such as water, liquor, tea, and coffee. But there are other things that one can *nomu*, such as medicine, and medicines do not have to be liquid; one can *nomu* medicine in powder or tablet form as well. *Nomu* is also used with reference to cigarettes, in which case it refers only to inhaling smoke.

From this analysis, a preliminary statement can be made: the Japanese verb *nomu* has an extremely wide range of objects, that is, the verb may be used for fluids, solids, and gases.

Next we will consider the conditions governing the use of the English verb *drink*, which is supposed to correspond to *nomu*. Certainly things one can drink include water, tea, coffee, and liquor. *Drink* may also be used for certain kinds of soup. Naturally, it cannot be used for solid food. One does not drink medicine in powder or pill form. For cigarettes, one says *smoke* rather than *drink*. Thus we come to realize, first of all, that *drink* can be used only when the object is a liquid.

However, this does not explain everything, because *drink* does not apply to all liquids. For example, medicine in liquid form is taken, not drunk. Furthermore, *drink* is not used for fluids that are not meant for drinking. Lighter fluid, ammonia, and other fluids for household use are often poisonous and may be fatal if children *nomu* them by mistake.

In the United States, bottles containing fluids of this sort are usually labeled "Fatal if swallowed," never "Fatal if drunk." In other words, medicine, poison, as well as fluids that are not meant to be drunk, do not call for the verb *drink* even if they are in liquid form.

At this point, one might wish to object that, in at least one instance, a very well-known figure did drink poison. In B. Jowett's English translation of *Phaedo*, Socrates is repeatedly described as preparing to drink the cup of hemlock. In this case, however, the use of *drink* is intended to convey the impression of Socrates taking the poison *as if it were* a liquid intended to be drunk; this is clearly demonstrated in the following passage.

> At the same time the attendant handed the
> cup to Socrates, who in the easiest and gentlest
> manner, without the least fear or change of
> color or feature, . . . took the cup. . . . Then he
> held his breath and drank off the poison quite
> readily and cheerfully.[1]

All these observations may be summarized in one general statement: *Drink* refers to an act of orally taking some liquid that is expected to help maintain one's physical well-being. This definition of *drink* completely covers all the correct uses of the verb, while at the same time it clearly shows the structural differences between *drink* and a group of other verbs such as *take*, *smoke*, and *swallow*, which can also refer to an act of orally introducing something into the body.

The traditional way of citing, as in dictionary descriptions, all the Japanese words that each partially correspond to *drink*, such as *nomu*, *toru*, and *nomikomu*, is misleading. Since in Japanese *nomu* may be used for poisons and medicines, and even for pins and rings which children might swallow by mistake, one is easily tempted to stretch the meaning of *drink* and apply it to all these situations. No matter how many example sentences are provided to show the various correct uses of the verb, there is a limit to what they can do. It will be difficult to prevent erroneous interpretations based on inappropriate generalizations.

The foregoing structural explanation of *drink* should also help us understand in greater detail the structural significance of the Japanese verb *nomu*, which may be defined as "to introduce a substance into one's body *without chewing it*." Rice is normally something to *taberu* 'eat,' but if a fish bone is stuck in someone's throat, we say, "You should *nomu* some rice." This demonstrates that *nomu*, unlike *drink*, has no restrictions at all as to the shape or the characteristics of the object, but focuses instead on the way it is taken, namely, without chewing.

Description of *Break*

Let us return now to *break*, which we discussed earlier. If we analyze its use by clarifying the conditions under which it may be used, it becomes immediately clear that *break*, first of all, means "to separate something into two or more parts by applying a sudden external force to it." (For the sake of simplicity, I am limiting my discussion here to the concrete use of the verb, but I hope this will in turn show the reader that the figurative use of *break* is based on roughly the same considerations.) The reason *break* is used for twigs, windowpanes, and electrical circuits (these things require different verbs in Japanese: *oru, kowasu,* and *kiru,* respectively) is that, in each case, some force is suddenly applied to an entity, separating it into two or more segments. It is for this reason that *break* may be used for arms and twigs, while *fold* is required for paper.

The Japanese verb *oru*, on the other hand, is similar to *break* in the sense of dividing an object into two sections by the application of external force, but it is different in that it does not necessarily require that the two resulting sections actually be separate from each other. Precisely for this reason, one can use *oru* for such things as wire and knees (where *bend* would be called for in English). Twigs and bones, for which *oru* is also used, separate in two simply because they happen to lack elasticity.

English has another important word that means "to separate something into two or more parts by applying force to it." This verb is *cut*. It differs structurally from *break* in that it may be used only for separating something by means of an instrument with a sharp edge. Thus it becomes clear why *break* is used instead of *cut* in English when we would say in Japanese, *Tsuyoi kaze no tame ni, densen ga kireta* (<*kireru*, lit., 'is cut') 'The power line broke because of the strong wind.' Japanese speakers of English would tend to use *cut* in such a case, but that is because neither *kiru* 'to cut something' nor *kireru* 'something is cut' necessarily presupposes the use of a sharp edge.

Thus it finally becomes clear that *break* means "to separate something into two or more parts by applying an external force other than an edged tool to it." If one understands *break* in this way, one will be able to determine confidently whether or not the verb could properly be used.

21

Overt Culture and Covert Culture

The culture of a country affects all aspects of the life and thought of the people living there. Like the presence of the atmosphere, it is something that is basically difficult for people who were born and have grown up in the midst of it to be conscious of. They take everything in their culture for granted; most of them go through their lives without realizing that there can be other ways of living or doing things.

Of course, in Japan today the media are well developed, more and more Japanese have had the experience of traveling abroad, and it is no longer unusual to see foreigners in our cities. As a result, most people know that customs, manners, and behavioral patterns vary from country to country. However, the cultural differences most easily noticed are usually limited to relatively obvious, concrete phenomena, i.e., to those aspects of culture which some scholars call "overt culture."

As an example of overt cultural differences, we can again refer to eating habits. Japanese eat with chopsticks while Occidentals use silverware. In Japan, people treat raw sea urchins and sea cucumbers as delicacies, but the same individuals cannot cope with blood sausages or sheep's brains if they encounter them while traveling in Europe. Thus, we all end up by saying to ourselves, "How can they eat things like that in other countries?" This is due to differences in overt culture.

In contrast to overt culture, that aspect of culture which is not easily visible and is therefore not readily noticeable is called "covert culture." Take eating utensils as an example. Nowadays the Japanese are accustomed to using

Westerner   Japanese

Figure 2

spoons and forks, and young people in particular can handle them as well as they can chopsticks. But if one observes carefully, their use of these utensils is slightly different from that of Occidentals. When a Japanese eats soup with a spoon, he lifts it to his mouth in a line parallel to his face. It follows therefore that he eats from the side of the spoon. Moreover, he sucks the liquid into his mouth, an action attributable to the traditional Japanese way of ingesting *suimono* 'Japanese soup,' which literally means "something to suck in."

An Occidental, on the other hand, lifts a spoon to his face at an angle close to ninety degrees and eats from the tip of the spoon, and, instead of sucking in the liquid, he pours it in with the tip of the spoon placed relatively deep in the mouth. In addition to this, there are other differences—in posture, in the distance between plate, mouth, and spoon— if we only look carefully enough.

Even though Japanese and Occidentals may be using the same cultural item, there are structural differences that are easily overlooked. Culture is composed of innumerable minute habitual behavior patterns, of which people them-selves are often unaware. Noticing this covert side is the key to understanding other cultures. One of the significant goals of foreign-language learning must also lie in this area.

A frequent complaint in recent years is that many years

23

of studying foreign languages in school does not seem to result in proficiency. But actually, one cannot expect, nor is it necessary, to be proficient in conversation or correspondence in a foreign language if one is not part of real life situations in which the language is used, especially if the teacher is not a native speaker of the language being taught. It is more important to teach the student how each language slices the world differently, each at different angles and in different ways. Indeed, this should be possible anywhere and for anybody. Unfortunately, classroom teachers have neglected this aspect of language more than one might imagine.

It Never Rains

I would now like to explain, taking an example from outside the vocabulary level, how the covert structure of one's native culture and language hinders one's understanding of a foreign language.

Among the English sayings sometimes taught in Japanese schools, there is one that goes "It never rains but it pours." Until several years ago, I simply assumed that it meant "Misfortunes occur in succession" or "Mishaps happen one after the other." In other words, I used to believe it was the equivalent of such Japanese proverbs as *Nakitsura ni hachi*, lit., 'a bee for a crying face' or *Fundari kettari*, lit., 'being stepped on and kicked at the same time,' because all English-Japanese dictionaries explain this proverb in more or less the same way, as follows:

Dai eiwajiten (Fuzanbō, 1951): (1) It never rains unless it pours. (2) Whenever it rains, it rains heavily. (3) Unlucky events always occur in succession.

Eiwa daijiten (Kenkyūsha, 1953): (proverb) Whenever it rains, it pours; mishaps and misfortunes come together.

Saishin concise eiwajiten (Sanseidō, 1958): (proverb) Whenever it rains, it pours; misfortunes occur in succession.

Shin crown eiwa jukugojiten (Sanseidō, 1966): When it rains, it pours; misfortunes follow one after another.

New world eiwajiten (Kodansha, 1969): Whenever it rains, it pours; misfortunes occur in succession.

Iwanami eiwa daijiten (Iwanami, 1970): Whenever it rains, it pours; mishaps come one after the other.

As demonstrated above, all the dictionaries first give a direct translation of the English proverb and then explain the meaning. The only two exceptions I found were *Shin-eiwa daijiten* (Kenkyūsha, 1928) and *Iwanami eiwajiten* (Iwanami, 1958), which quote *Nakitsura ni hachi* as a correponding Japanese proverb.

One day I happened to look up this proverb in Harrap's *Standard English and French Dictionary*, which I rarely use, to see how it was explained in French. To my surprise, I found the following explanation under *rain*: "un malheur, un bonheur, ne vient jamais seul; jamais deux sans trois; quand on reçoit une visite, une lettre, on en reçoit dix." I was shocked to discover that this proverb might also refer to *bonheur* 'good luck,' since I had assumed until then that it could be used for nothing but a succession of misfortunes.

I hastened to consult several Oxford dictionaries and was again shocked to find, under the entry for *pour*, the following explanations:

Oxford English Dictionary: events (esp. misfortunes) come all together or happen in rapid succession.

25

Shorter Oxford Dictionary: same as above.

Concise Oxford Dictionary (3rd ed., 1937; 4th ed., 1952; 5th ed., 1964): (fig.) events, esp. misfortunes, always come together.

Pocket Oxford Dictionary (1934): events, esp. misfortune, come many together.

Although they all insert "esp. misfortunes," they do not clearly exclude a succession of happy or lucky events. Oxford dictionaries are considered the most authoritative in the world; *OED*, in particular, is regarded by scholars of English as the ultimate authority with respect to English. It is hardly conceivable that Japanese dictionary editors in the past have never consulted any of the four mentioned.

Utterly shocked, I proceeded to consult another well-known British dictionary, *Universal English Dictionary*, only to find under *rain*: "things, events, never happen or come singly but always in numbers together." This interpretation makes no distinction between unlucky and lucky events.

Although I had already treated this whole story in a previous article,[2] I renewed my investigation and discovered an even more interesting fact, namely, that in the *Concise Oxford Dictionary*, the same proverb appears not only under *pour*, but also under *rain*. Moreover, the explanation under *rain* is slightly different (in both the third and the fourth editions): "events usually happen several together." As it turns out, then, the interpretation including lucky as well as unlucky events was in an Oxford dictionary after all.

I went a step further and looked at several American dictionaries, but did not find this proverb in any of the three Webster's dictionaries I consulted, nor did I find it in the *American College Dictionary*, the new *Random House Dictionary* or the *American Heritage Dictionary*. This convinced me anew of American dictionaries' emphasis on the explanation of things rather than of words.

My investigation leads to one conclusion. The proverb, rather than meaning "Misfortunes come in succession" or *Nakitsura ni hachi*, corresponds exactly to the Japanese proverb *Nido aru koto wa sando*, lit., 'Events that happen twice happen three times.' It is really the equivalent of another English proverb, "What happens twice will happen thrice."

What caused the one-sided interpretation I discovered in all the Japanese dictionaries? An unkind supposition that one of the earliest editors of English-Japanese dictionaries made a hasty misinterpretation of this proverb, which later editors have simply been copying ever since, may not be totally wrong. However, anyone who had ever consulted a British dictionary would have noticed this error. It is very unlikely that no one has ever done this.[3]

My hypothesis, however, is that the way the Japanese subconsciously react unfavorably to the word *rain*, or especially *pour*, narrowed the original meaning of this proverb. Although we do have some Japanese expressions showing a favorable attitude toward rain, such as *kanten no jiu* 'long-awaited rain after a spell of hot dry weather,' the image of rain reflected in more common expressions, such as *ame ni furareru* 'be unfavorably affected by a rainfall,' and particularly *doshaburi ni au* 'be caught in a downpour,' is a gloomy and unpleasant one. Would it be too wild to speculate that the negative attitude Japanese have towards rain led to this misinterpretation?

A Rolling Stone

To illustrate how strong the tendency to interpret foreign words and expressions in the context of one's own culture is, I would like to cite one more proverb: "A rolling stone gathers no moss." This proverb (usually translated into Japanese as *Tenseki koke o shōzezu*) is explained in the *Concise Oxford Dictionary* as meaning "One who constantly changes his place of employment will not grow rich." This is obviously a proverb warning against lack of perseverance.

In America, however, this saying is sometimes taken to mean the exact opposite.[4] For instance, a young American man I know explained its meaning to me as "If you keep on moving and being active, you will not get rusty." This interpretation clearly demonstrates that, with regard to the notions of moss and changing jobs, people in the New World have a different sense of values than do the British.

Most Americans do not care for things like old weather-beaten houses. They constantly repaint and frequently renovate their houses. After World War II, when many Japanese houses were requisitioned by the occupation forces, we often heard about old unpainted wooden alcove posts receiving a coat of paint from the new American residents. I also know of an American living in a Japanese house who had taken a wire brush and polished clean a moss-covered stone lantern in the yard. These incidents made it clear to me that Americans consider moss something dirty and unpleasant, like rust. In this, their sense of values differs from that of Europeans.

In American society, changing jobs frequently is often regarded as rather desirable for individual development.

Social mobility has a positive value there. Americans even say that mobility proves ability. This is the cultural background which leads them to give "A rolling stone gathers no moss" an interpretation exactly opposite to the one prevalent in England.

2. Things and Words

Correspondence

Think about what a huge number of "things" surround our lives. As I sit writing this, I see on my desk a desk lamp, a typewriter, an ashtray, books, letters, a writing pad, a ball-point pen, an eraser, a lighter, and pencils lying about in disarray. The drawers of the desk are packed with scores of articles such as stationery, thumbtacks, scissors, keys, a stapler, a knife, and a bundle of calling cards. I myself am wearing many more objects than I can count on my fingers —a suit, a sweater, a necktie, a white shirt, socks, glasses, a wristwatch, a belt, and so on. Once we start thinking in this way about the kinds of products we humans have created and use daily, we realize the incredible variety they represent. In the realm of nature, too, there are tens of thousands of species of birds and beasts. The insect world is known to comprise hundreds of thousands of different species. In addition, there are a tremendous number of plants. Each species has a name of its own.

It is not only concrete objects that have names. The movements of objects and the motions of human beings, even subtle shifts in our mental states are all matched with words. The characteristics of things—and the relationships between things—are assigned appropriate words to express them. Just trying to imagine how many kinds of things, both concrete and abstract, might exist in the world is staggering.

Besides, the number of objects and of words corresponding to a certain object often exceeds the sum total. Take, for example, the automobile. Although it is only one object, it is composed of about twenty thousand parts, each of which, quite naturally, has a name. A jet airplane is said to require hundreds of thousands of parts. To make the matter more complicated, the parts may be even further subdivided. Many are made of different materials, which in turn have different components, each of which has its own name, and so on. Thus it is that things and words, in mutual correspondence, trap man in the fine meshes of their netting. Nothing is nameless. Everything in the universe has a name. That must be our simple yet firm conviction.

An equally firm conviction is the belief of most people that the name of a particular object varies completely from country to country and from language to language. A dog, for example, is called by various names: *inu* in Japanese, *kou* in Chinese, *chien* in French, *Hund* in German, *sobaka* in Russian, and *köpek* in Turkish. When we study a foreign language at school or consult a dictionary to see what the equivalent of a particular word is in another language, we do so on the basic premise that the same object will just require a different word in a different language.

Words Create Things

Some philosophers and linguists, however, who study the relationship between words and things doubt the validity of this premise. After examining the relations between various words and objects and studying the question of the same object being named differently in each language, I have also come to have similar doubts. Most people hold that objects exist independently of language and that words are then devised as labels for them, but I believe, on the contrary, that words create things. Furthermore, despite the common belief that the identical object merely wears a different label in different languages, one should view the difference in name not only as a difference in label; in fact, different names represent considerably different things, although the extent of the difference may vary from case to case.

The first of the two points made just above—the idea that words create things, and not the converse—has been a topic of philosophical argument since ancient times. The labels given these two opposing positions are nominalism and realism. I am going to argue, from a purely linguistic standpoint, that nominalism explains the structure of language more accurately. My argument may be summarized in a single phrase: "In the beginning was the Word."

I do not, of course, mean that at the birth of the universe, when emptiness prevailed, words alone existed. Moreover, when I say that words create things, I do not mean that words bring forth objects as hens lay eggs. I mean, rather, that we recognize fragments of the universe as objects or properties only through words, and that without words we could not even distinguish dogs from cats.

If words are the key to our understanding of the universe and the only window through which to perceive it, what we perceive must also vary to some extent, depending on the structure and system of the language we use. The reason is, as I will explain in detail below, that language is nothing but a device with which to determine what parts or properties, from among those impressions impinging on our senses, we should focus our attention on when we try to understand the world in an orderly way. I have just used the metaphor that words are the window through which to perceive the world, but if the size and the shape of the window and the color and refraction of the pane vary, the extent and nature of the perceived world will naturally differ. One may not even see an object if there is no appropriate word for it.

An Arbitrarily Segmented World

I should put a stop to abstract argument here and turn to some concrete linguistic facts. Let us begin by taking a *tsukue* 'desk *or* table' as an example of a commonplace object. What is this thing called a *tsukue*? How should it be defined? A *tsukue* is sometimes made of wood, sometimes of steel. In the summer, some people use glass ones in their yards; in parks we even find concrete ones. The number of legs a *tsukue* has also varies. For example, the one I am using now has no legs because it is built-in, attached to the wall. While there are one-legged *tsukue*, there are also many-legged ones such as those used for conferences. These are usually oblong, square, or round, but there are also triangular *tsukue*, the kind placed in the corner of a room on which a vase might be placed. In height, they range from low ones used without chairs in Japanese-style rooms to high ones used with chairs.

From this analysis, it becomes clear that we can hardly define a *tsukue* on the basis of concrete external characteristics such as shape, material, color, size, or number of legs. If we must, nonetheless, try to define a *tsukue*, a possible definition might be "an object which provides a surface on which to do something." The shape, size, and material of a particular *tsukue* in a given country at a given time will, within a certain predictable range, be determined by the conditions that make it necessary to provide that kind of surface in a certain area. Various restrictions imposed on the commercial production of the article may also influence its design.

But then, are all surfaces on which we do something *tsukue*? Not necessarily. For example, the definition given for *tsukue* also applies to a shelf. A floor also belongs to the same category in the sense that we do something on it. In order to distinguish *tsukue* from shelves and floors, we must change our definition to "a surface that is detached from the floor, and on which one does something while sitting or standing in front of it for a certain period of time."

I would like the reader to note that the important part of this long-winded definition is the human element, that is, the practical use which a person makes of the object, or its relative position vis-à-vis a person. Although a *tsukue* is made from materials that exist apart from man, their many properties do not contribute to the definition of the object referred to by the word *tsukue*. If we detach ourselves from our human perspective and look around a room as if through the eyes of a pet dog or cat, we will not be able to distinguish a *tsukue* from some types of shelves or chairs. A *tsukue* is a *tsukue* due to man's particular viewpoint. And the power of language is what makes us think that a *tsukue* is there.

Thus one function of language is to divide the chaotic world of nonentities into fictitious segments and to classify them according to human perspective in a way significant to us. Language intrinsically contains a fictitious quality whereby it presents to man the ever-growing, ever-changing world as groups of neatly subdivided objects. We often hear the common expression "the magic of language," but apart from the commonplace implication of this expression, language is indeed magic. It may even be a binding curse in that it leads us to mistake this dynamic world for a static one.

Let us return to the consideration of concrete examples from language, this time taking up entities that exist in the world of nature instead of such manufactured products as desks and tables.

Linguistic Relativity

The novelist D. H. Lawrence once wrote a short story entitled "Prelude." In it there is a description of a woman making tea.

> . . . and catching up the blue enameled teapot,
> [she] dropped into it a handful of tea from the
> caddy, and poured on the water.

Japanese readers unfamiliar with English customs may think that because customs vary from country to country, tea must be made with cold water in England. Others who have learned in school that the Japanese word *yu* corresponds to *hot water* in English, may suspect that in the passage above *hot* in *hot water* must have been left out by mistake. Neither interpretation, of course, is correct.

English people are world famous for their love of tea. They are fastidious about tea making. In particular, they demand that tea be made with boiling water. Some people even go so far as to warn, "Don't carry the kettle to the teapot. Carry the teapot to the kettle." Moreover, warming the teapot in advance with a cup of hot water is only common sense to the English. For them, it would be totally unthinkable to make tea with cold water.

The British attitude toward tea is vividly described in the following passage from Agatha Christie's mystery *A Pocket Full of Rye*. Here, a newly hired typist, a spiritless and slovenly woman called Somers, is making tea in the office. She is being scolded by the head typist, long an employee of the firm.

> The kettle was not quite boiling when Miss
> Somers poured the water on the tea . . . . Miss
> Griffith, the efficient head typist, . . . said
> sharply: "Water not boiling again, Somers!"

As is clear from these two examples, in English there is actually no single-word equivalent of *yu* 'hot water.' The English word *water* may mean either *mizu* 'cold water' or *yu*, depending on the context.

Of course, in English, it is possible to say *hot water* when it is necessary to make a clear distinction between hot and cold water. But the fact that *hot* has to be deliberately added to *water* in this way indicates that the word *water* in itself has a neutral quality with regard to temperature.

On the other hand, *mizu* in Japanese distinctly implies cool or cold water. *Atsui mizu*, literally 'hot cold water,' sounds unnatural because it is as self-contradictory as saying *a square triangle*. In everyday Japanese, the material expressed by the chemical formula H_2O has three distinctive names: *kōri* 'ice,' *mizu* 'cold water,' and *yu* 'hot water.' English, however, has only two names, *ice* and *water*, instead of three, and Malay has only one, *ayĕr*. This is shown graphically in table 1.

	H_2O		
Malay	ayĕr		
English	ice	water	
Japanese	kōri 'ice'	mizu 'cold water'	yu 'hot water'

Table 1

In Malay, one could say *ayĕr panas* 'hot water' to signify specifically the idea of *yu*, but this is merely the equivalent of *hot water* in English. One could also say *ayĕr beku* 'solidified water' if one wished to clearly distinguish ice from water, but *ayĕr* by itself may also be used for *ice*. These words from three different languages referring to H_2O in different ways are often cited as a good illustration of how differently and arbitrarily each language slices the objective world.

If a person has lived in one language environment all his life, he tends to take the correspondence between things and words more or less for granted; he hardly looks at it with suspicion. Only by comparing one's language with others in the above fashion does one begin to understand that even such commonplace words as *mizu*, *yu*, and *kōri* actually represent arbitrary subdivisions dependent for their very existence on the particular language called Japanese.

Bringing Order to the World

Cold water, hot water, and ice are three separate, independent entities in the minds of the Japanese because we project on the world of phenomena a linguistic system which distinctly separates *mizu, yu* and *kōri* from one another, treating each as an independent item.

It should be clear to everyone that the distinction between *mizu* and *yu* is based on a slight difference in temperature and is therefore merely a relative one. Between *kōri* and *mizu* (or *yu*), on the other hand, there is indeed an obvious distinction: one is a solid while the other is a fluid (although the difference can, in the final analysis, be explained in terms of temperature). Some people may wish to insist that the distinction between the two is not merely linguistic, but is rather attributable to an objective and visible difference which justifies it. But if this is so, what can we say about the distinction between *kōri* 'ice' and *tsurara* 'icicle'? The same substance ordinarily called *kōri* acquires the name *tsurara* in Japanese under certain limited conditions (in terms of location and shape). The substance itself undergoes no change. In other words, that which distinguishes these two items are the two words *kōri* and *tsurara*, which were assigned to two different ways of looking at one and the same object. It is not so strange, then, that in Turkey, where icicles do indeed exist, there should be no special word for them and that they are called simply *buz* 'ice.' Turks just do not see icicles as anything other than ice.

Pursuing this line of reasoning, we find that the lines of demarcation made in Japanese between *kōri* 'ice,' *hyō* 'large hailstone,' *arare* 'small hailstone,' *yuki* 'snow,' and *mizore* 'sleet' also become unclear, since all these things turn into rain when the temperature rises. The differences between *ame* 'rain,' *kasumi* 'haze,' and *moya* 'mist,' too, are based merely on the size of drops of water; moreover, they can all become clouds, depending on relative distance from the ground.

Why are these natural phenomena, each composed of the same elements, given different names? Because it is more convenient for us in our daily rounds to have labels for certain parts of our environment. Giving something a name simply means that we have recognized the value of treating one portion of the world separately from all the other sections and fragments. The same object that can be summed up in a chemical formula as H_2O is called by tens of different names in Japanese, ranging from *kōri*, *mizu*, *yu*, and *yuge* 'steam' to *tsuyu* 'dew' and *shimo* 'frost,' as well as *harusame* 'spring rain' and *yūdachi* 'late afternoon shower.' One cannot conclude, however, that H_2O is the only word which represents something certain while all the other words are names which do not refer to real objects, representing fictional entities with no substantial counterparts in the real world.

Even the term H_2O is something born out of man's effort to organize his world from one particular angle and is therefore nothing ultimate or definite. Obviously H_2O is hydrogen and oxygen combined in a particular configuration. One must in turn analyze these elements in terms of even more minute components, repeating the subdividing process. Thus, the object represented by the sign H_2O, a scientific term, shares the same fictitious quality as *tsurara* 'icicle' and *samidare* 'early summer rain.' All the words coined by man as he responds to the universe around him are based on this same arbitrariness.

39

Man cannot come into direct contact with the elements composing his world as such. These elements constitute a world meaningless in itself, one which might aptly be described as disorderly and chaotic. One must conclude that the role of language is to bring order to this world and fashion in it meaningful and controllable objects, properties, and actions.

Lip versus *Kuchibiru*

At the beginning of this chapter, I mentioned that man-made objects such as automobiles and airplanes are composed of a great number of parts, each of which has a name of its own. The human body may also be considered in the same way since it too consists of different parts with different names. A car has four wheels, two doors, and two head-lights. A person can be described as having two legs, two arms, a face with two eyes, one nose, and so on. It is impossible to think of even one part of the body that does not have a name. I am sure that even the tiniest bones and muscles have names given them by anatomists.

This may lead one to believe that, just as the automobile is composed of about twenty thousand parts with different names, the human body is also the sum total of thousands of parts, each with a name of its own. But there is actually a great difference between them.

To begin with, automobile parts are all obviously independent of and separate from one another but the parts of the human body are all connected. For example, even though we say there are eyes, a nose, and a mouth in the face, they are not really marked by clear boundaries. Everyone realizes that cheeks and jaws are different parts of the face, but no one knows where the line of demarcation lies. Eyes and lips may at first seem to be more clearly marked off than are cheeks and jaws, but upon closer examination we see that even this is a misconception.

Let us consider another example from the English language. John Galsworthy once wrote a short story about tragic love, "The Apple Tree." Many Japanese are familiar with it since it is often used in Japan in college-level textbooks. At the beginning of the story, the facial features of Ashurst, one of the main characters, are described in the following way:

> Ashurst, rather like a bearded Schiller, grey
> in the wings, . . . with . . . bearded lips just
> open.

If we translated *bearded lips* literally as *hige no haeta kuchibiru*, it would sound funny to thoughtful readers, because in Japanese *kuchibiru* normally refers only to the two red areas surrounding the mouth. They cannot possibly grow any hair!

A little further on, we come to a passage about the face of the heroine, Megan:

> Her face was short, her upper lip short, show-
> ing a glint of teeth.

Although we Japanese talk about the thickness or the thinness of a *kuchibiru*, the expression "a short *kuchibiru*" would be quite abnormal. We would be at a loss to figure out the shape of such a *kuchibiru*.

These two quotations about lips show that in English *lips* can refer to not only the protruding, distinctively colored areas outlining the mouth but also to a fairly large area surrounding them. The term *upper lip*, in particular, often seems to refer to the section which would be called *hana no shita* 'under the nose' in Japanese. It is this section of the face that Galsworthy has in mind when he describes Megan's upper lip as short. It is now clear why, if the upper lip is short, a glint of teeth is visible.

I began studying English over thirty years ago. I have also spent several years in the United States and Canada. Nevertheless, believe it or not, I only became aware of the difference between *lip* and *kuchibiru* two or three years ago! Needless to say, this difference is not mentioned in any dictionary that I have consulted, nor has any scholar of English or English literature whom I have asked shown any clear awareness of this.

However, now that I am aware of the difference, I take note of more and more examples. I often come across them in stories as I reread them. In Saroyan's "Seventeen," for instance, there is a "small woman of fifty with hair on her upper lip"; in Agatha Christie's *The Labors of Hercules*, the famous sleuth Poirot has an "immense mustache that adorned his upper lip." In short, the place where a mustache grows is called the *lip* in English.

I once wrote an article about this particular discovery and published it in a linguistics magazine. Afterwards, I received letters from many readers reporting more findings of the same nature, including examples from German, French, and Italian. My friend and colleague, Noboru Fujii, a classical Latin scholar, kindly provided me with the following interesting example from Martial:

iam mihi nigrescunt tonsa sudaria barba

et queritur labris puncta puella meis.

(Mart. XI, xxxix, 3–4)

This passage is about a young man who is always teased by everyone for being childish. He protests that even he finds the scarf around his neck black with bits of hair after each shave, and that when he kisses his girl, she complains angrily about how much his lip stings her because of his mustache. This poem shows clearly that in ancient Rome, too, a mustache grew on the upper lip.

Two Levels of Understanding

Our discussion of *lip* and *kuchibiru* may be summarized as follows. First, even with regard to such seemingly clear-cut parts of the human face as lips, each language possesses a term with a different range of meaning. Second, some languages do not have a word specifically referring to the area immediately under the nose. Third, despite the discrepancy in range of meaning between *kuchibiru* in Japanese and *lip* in English, many scholars of English have failed to notice it. And finally, our failure to notice this difference apparently has not affected our comprehension of what we hear or read.

The first point above means that *kuchibiru* belongs only to Japanese, and that *lip* refers to part of the face which exists only in the eyes of English-speaking people. Since *lip* and *kuchibiru* are not identical in meaning, one cannot argue that an object initially existed independently of individual languages and was later labeled *kuchibiru* in Japanese, and *lip* in English.

The second point merely states that every single part of

43

the body will not necessarily have a name in every language.

The third point tells us that although it is not really difficult for the student of a foreign language to reach a certain level of proficiency in terms of understanding what he hears or reads or of making himself understood in the language, minute differences in the meanings of words between the student's native language and the target language are not grasped as correctly as one might expect.

The last point suggests that when we read a foreign language, we are really thinking in our native language most of the time. We are helped by the logic of the subject or the context in which the word occurs. When a Japanese comes across the expression *bearded lips*, therefore, he does not take it to mean "*kuchibiru* covered with hair," but understands it correctly as "hair around the mouth." But his understanding takes place through Japanese, which explains why he will never use such an expression when he writes English, and why he will not remember ever having seen it used.

Vague Reference

While talking about the face, I wish to discuss the eyes and the nose as well. Cheeks and jaws are rather difficult to define. But surely no reader would suspect that eyes might be equally hard to define. Contrary to expectation, however, eyes are actually very vague areas also.

To clarify this point, I will list five uses of *brick* and *eyes*, respectively.

1 This brick is rectangular.	1′ His eyes are round.
2 This brick is red.	2′ His eyes are blue.

3 This brick is heavy.	3′ His eyes are large.
4 This brick is hard.	4′ His eyes are good.
5 This brick is chipped.	5′ His eyes are sunken.

Examples 1 through 5 are sentences about several characteristics of a given brick; sentences 1′ through 5′ are various attempts to describe someone's eyes.

Sentences 1 through 5 are all descriptions about the same referent. In them, the relationship between the word *brick* and the referent remains unchanged. On the other hand, in sentences 1′ through 5′, which are structurally quite similar to the former group, the relationship between the word *eyes* and its referent varies significantly. *Eyes* in 1′ refers to the shape of the eyes as outlined by the upper and lower eyelids, and not to the roundness of the eyeballs. In 2′, *eyes* refers to the irises. Sentence 3′ is a comment on the size of the portion of the eyeballs that is exposed between the upper and lower eyelids, while sentence 4′ is about "his" eyesight. In sentence 5′, the eyeballs themselves are not sunken; what is described here is the location of the eyes in relation to the surface planes of the face.

When one says "a chipped brick," one means that a part of the brick is missing. Likewise, *red*, *heavy*, *hard*, and *rectangular* are all descriptions of the brick itself. In comparison, the way the referent of the word *eyes* changes each time is indeed amazing. What part of the head does the word *eye* really refer to?

When one compares the names for the parts of the human face with one another, *eye* at first seems more easily definable than such words as *cheek* and *temple*. However, when one tries to focus on the eyes, what exactly constitutes them suddenly becomes less clear.

Discrepancies in Areas of Meaning

What about the nose? I stated earlier that certain languages lack words specifically referring to the area under the nose. However, probably no language lacks a word referring to the nose itself. But even the nose is not free of problems.

First of all, the thing called *hana* 'nose' in Japanese is an entity whose full range of meaning is only appreciated by Japanese speakers. Of course, this does not mean that the part of the face referred to as *hana* is lacking in others; non-Japanese speakers are all possessed of *hana*. Furthermore, in Japanese, we also say that the elephant has a long *hana* 'trunk.' To the Japanese speaker, the object hanging down from the elephant's head and the object located in the middle

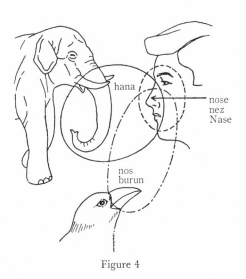

Figure 4

of the human face are both *hana*. In other words, they are members of the same category, the category called *hana*.

In many other languages, however, the thing projecting out of the elephant's face and the one protruding from the human face cannot be called by the same name. In English, for example, the elephant's *hana* is called a *trunk*, as though it belonged to the same category as the trunk of a tree. It is called *trompe* in French and *Rüssel* in German, and is thus differentiated from the human nose, which is called *nez* in the former and *Nase* in the latter. Interestingly enough, *burun* in Turkish and *nos* in Russian may refer to both the human nose and the beak of a bird. In other words, each language has a word for the projection in the middle of the human face, but its range of meaning varies. In this sense, the range of objects that may be referred to by the Japanese word *hana* is peculiar to the Japanese language.

Another problem is that even adjectives used to describe the nose exhibit a great deal of variability from one language to another. I have already discussed this subject elsewhere,[1] so I touch on it here only briefly. Although we describe human noses in Japanese as *takai* 'high' or *hikui* 'low,' the same adjectives we use for mountains, this is rarely the case in other languages.

According to the usage of European languages today, noses may be large or small, or long or short, but are usually not high or low—like mountains. Turkish also uses its equivalents of *long* and *short* to describe noses. In Japanese, on the other hand, we use *nagai* 'long' and *mijikai* 'short' for noses only on limited occasions, as, for example, in reference to the protagonist in Ryūnosuke Akutagawa's short story "Hana," who agonized over his ugly nose. But normally noses are de-

47

scribed as *takai* 'high' or *hikui* 'low.' The nose of the imaginary Japanese creature *tengu* 'a long-nosed goblin,' too, is *takai* 'high,' not *nagai* 'long.'

I once treated this problem on the assumption that Japanese culture is extremely nose-oriented. Since then I have noticed linguistic facts which support this view. In Japanese novels, the protagonist's first appearance, if accompanied by a detailed description of his face, invariably includes some information on the nose as well as on the eyes, the mouth, and the eyebrows.

In English novels, however, I have discovered that even when a face is described in detail, there is scant reference to the nose. To illustrate, let me call once more on Agatha Christie's detective M. Poirot:

> Hercule Poirot looked thoughtfully into the face of the man behind the big mahogany desk. He noted that generous brow, the mean mouth, the rapacious lines of the jaw, and the piercing visionary eyes. (Agatha Christie: *The Labors of Hercules*)

The famous detective, who never overlooks even the smallest detail, is studying a man's face here, trying to deduce what kind of man he is by observing his eyebrows, his mouth, the shape of his jaw, and the look in his eyes. Nevertheless there is no reference to the nose. I wonder if Japanese authors describing the face of a character under similar circumstances would disregard the nose.

Cultural Selection

Naturally this does not mean that the nose plays no role

in European literature. There are such famous examples as Rostand's *Cyrano De Bergerac* and Gogol's *Nose*. In both cases, however, the subject is a nose that is too large, cumbersome, and ugly. Generally speaking, when there is a reference to the nose of a character in a European novel, it is often to an ugly nose regarded as a flaw. It seems to me that Europeans and Americans regard the nose as something repulsive.

In other cases, the nose is mentioned as a racial characteristic. For example, "She had . . . the slightly flattened nose of the Slav" (Agatha Christie: *The Seven Dials Mystery*).

The tendency not to pay much attention to the nose is found both in European and in Turkish literatures. A Turkish short story writer Ömer Seyyfetin once wrote a story with the curious title "Human Nature and the Dog." In one scene, a first-class passenger boards a ship in Istanbul and wonders about another passenger, a beautiful woman with a dog, sitting forlornly apart from the crowd. He describes her face.

> İnce, uzun kaşlar, solgun ve asabî bir çehre, ciddî kadınlara hâs, meselâ muallime, rahibe gibi, bir hüsn-i lâtif, bir hüsn-i mahrun. . . . Siyah gözleri altın bir gözlüğün camları arkasından daha parlıyor gibi görünüyordu.

> Long thin eyebrows, a pale, nervous-looking face with a kind of refreshing but lonely beauty characteristic of serious women such as teachers and nuns. . . . With dark eyes shining even more brightly through gold-rimmed glasses.

The description continues in this way, but there is no mention of her mouth, let alone her nose.

Let me cite one more example, from a short story by the

same author entitled "The Secret of Ugliness." In it, the hero describes the face of a matchless beauty thus:

> Bence İstanbulun en güzel kızı odur! Siyah, iri, parlak gözler. . . . Gür siyah saçlar. . . . Sonra inanılmaz derecede saf bir beyazlık! Mukaddes bir rüya beyazlığı!
>
> In my opinion, she is the most beautiful girl in Istanbul! Large, shiny dark eyes. . . . Rich, soft black hair. . . . And incredible fair skin with pure, dreamlike whiteness.

Here, too, the nose and the mouth are disregarded. These two ladies from Turkish stories are portrayed as modern women in Western clothes wearing European-style hairdos; of course their noses and mouths are perfectly visible since they are not wearing the veils traditionally worn by Muslim women.

In Turkey, Islam was recognized as the state religion until about half a century ago, and it still exerts a strong influence on the country, especially in rural areas. For five hundred years after the Turkish nation was converted to Islam, the Islamic way of thinking, with its minute rules and regulations, governed all aspects of national life. It is only natural that even in the Republic of Turkey, which today is on the road to modernization and Westernization, such a long-established view of things should still remain in the minds of the people, though not necessarily in the same form as before.

While Islam was Turkey's state religion, it was considered a taboo for women to show their faces to men other than their closest relatives. Even today, some old women, though they may not usually wear veils, suddenly raise them with their hands to hide their faces as soon as they see a tourist approaching. In a country with such customs, it is no wonder that female beauty has come to be judged only by certain limited parts of the head exposed to others—the eyes, the eyebrows, the forehead, the color of whatever facial skin is visible, and the hair.

However, in every culture, the choice of criteria for female beauty usually belongs to covert culture and therefore regulates a person's judgment without entering his consciousness. The fact that Turkish authors do not mention a woman's nose or mouth when describing her face might be due to cultural constraints. Beauty is still sought only within the traditional framework. Human eyes do not see things objectively and impartially like cameras. Our perceptions are always subject to cultural selection.

Chins and Jaws

While doing research on different ways of describing faces, I have come to notice another interesting fact. That is, in English novels much attention is paid to the chins and the jaws of the characters. For example:

> She had pale blue, rather vacant-looking eyes, and a *weak indeterminate* chin. She had a long upper lip. (A. Christie: *A Pocket Full of Rye*. Italics added.)

Such adjectives as *weak* and *indeterminate* are probably not used very often by Japanese writers in reference to chins and jaws. In English novels, however, similar examples can be easily found if one only starts looking: "the *rapacious* lines of the jaw" (A. Christie: *The Labors of Hercules*), "She was a vigorous looking woman of sixty-odd, with iron-grey hair and a *determined* chin" (A. Christie: *Mrs. McGinty's Dead*). A chin may be described as "the small square *fighting* chin" (A. Christie: *Crooked House*). There are chins which are *indecisive* or *pugnacious* and jaws which are *ruthless* or *aggressive*.

These adjectives refer primarily to the characters of the persons to whom particular chins or jaws belong. In other words, the chin and the jaw are seen as parts of a person by which his vitality, personality, will power, determination or the lack thereof can be judged.

In contrast, descriptions of chins and jaws by Japanese incline much more toward visual shapes. For example, we say in Japanese that someone has a wide or square jaw, a concave, long, pointed, or double (this last adjective is used in English, too) chin, or simply no chin at all. All these frequently used descriptions pertain to external appearances. We appear rarely to consider the chin and the jaw as parts of the face which reveal one's character.

Eijirō Iwasaki, a scholar of German, has told me that, in German, chins are sometimes described as *stark* 'strong,' *brutal* 'brutal,' or *energisch* 'energetic.' Hideichi Matsubara, a scholar of French, has pointed out to me the French expression *mâchoire volontaire* 'strong-willed jaw.' Judging from these examples, the association of the chin and jaw with one's character, spirit, etc., might be the common thing in European cultures.

While considering this problem, I happened to leaf through Michitarō Tada's *Shigusa no Nihon bunka* [Japanese gestures and Japanese culture] and came across the following passage:

Europeans unconsciously stick out their chins to take an aggressive posture. They could not survive in this tough world otherwise. Japanese, on the contrary, pull in their chins to assume a low posture. A Frenchman living in Japan once observed this and asked the interesting question why the Japanese pull in their chins.

To support Tada's view, the following sentence may be cited as an example:

Pennington's jaw hardened. He shot out his chin at them aggressively. (A. Christie: *Death on the Nile*)

There is also the idiom used in America, *keep one's chin up,* which means "not to be discouraged." In Japanese, on the other hand, *to stick out one's chin* means "to be totally exhausted."

If I may digress, the fact that in boxing, a sport developed in Europe, one is supposed to attack the opponent's chin persistently may have something to do with the European view that a man's chin is the source of his vitality. In fist-fighting, too, Europeans readily strike each other on the chin, whereas we Japanese hit the opponent on the head or slap him on the cheek.

To reiterate my point, although the human face is common to all races and all cultures and is a very conspicuous part of the body, the structure of vocabulary items for its parts varies greatly from language to language. This is because the way people view a particular part of the face, as well as the value they assign to it, differs from culture to culture. Even the adjectives used to describe a particular facial feature may be completely different.

After considering all these points, it seems to me linguistically more appropriate to conclude thus: man does not use words to describe things which exist in the objective world; rather words, which reflect a particular view of the world or a specific way of dissecting it, make us feel as though objects with such characteristics and properties actually exist.

3. Adjectives

Adjectival Categories

In the preceding chapter I considered the relationship between words and things mainly with reference to nouns, that is, to the names given to concrete objects. In this chapter, I wish to take up adjectives, the words which refer to properties and characteristics of things.

My examination of nouns unexpectedly revealed that what have so far been regarded as substantive entities are actually viewed in a strongly subjective light, and are created out of necessity by man, the perceiver. The same holds true for adjectives. For example, the expressions *a faraway country* and *a nearby country*, at first glance, look exactly the same structurally as *a strong country* and *a weak country*. One therefore tends to assume that in the former pair, as in the latter, the adjectives describe properties or conditions of certain countries. However, a little careful thinking helps one realize that this is not the case.

The adjectives *faraway* and *nearby* merely refer to the relative distance between a certain object and the speaker. For this reason, a faraway country gradually becomes a nearby country as one travels in that direction. In contrast, a strong country remains strong regardless of its distance from the speaker. The belief that both adjectives in the expression *a strong faraway country* make statements about the nature of a country is a misconception caused by a similarity in grammatical use.

The adjective *unusual* also has a strange semantic structure. For example, the shapes of Japanese dishes are usually square, rectangular, or round; triangular dishes are very uncommon. If, therefore, someone who likes unconventional things makes triangular dishes, they may sell at a high price as "unusual" items. However, triangles themselves are obviously nothing unusual. In fact, if a great quantity of triangular dishes were produced for sale, they would immediately cease to be unusual despite the fact that the properties of the dishes do not change at all.

It is evident from this example that being unusual is not a property inherent to the object modified by the adjective. *Unusual* means that the objects referred to do not exist in great numbers, that there are few items of the same kind. Nevertheless, when one hears about an "unusual little red bird," one tends to imagine that the bird must have an uncommon property.

There are many adjectives with such unexpected meanings as the ones above. Since it is impossible to discuss them all here, let me concentrate on the hitherto little-studied structure of a particular group of adjectives.

Relative Adjectives and Absolute Adjectives

In each language, there are pairs of antonymous adjectives such as *long-short*, *large-small*, and *high-low* which describe things in terms of various dimensions. Actually, upon closer examination, one notices some inconsistencies. For example,

French has *profond* 'deep' but no specific word to express its opposite. *Altus* in Latin signals a vertical distance not only above the point of reference, as in Japanese *takai* 'high,' but also below the point of reference, somewhat like Japanese *fukai* 'deep'; it may therefore be used both for the deep root of a tree as well as for a high mountain. But here I am not dealing with such discrepancies that complicate the issue.

Now, the reason I wish to discuss such pairs as *long-short* and *large-small* is that although these adjectives may give the impression of describing the shapes of certain objects, in absolute terms, they actually are semantically based on an implicit comparison of these objects with something else.

For example, *large* and *red* in *a large red apple* may seem to express two properties of a certain apple on equal terms. However, the structural difference between the two can be easily seen through this simple experiment. Suppose there is someone who has never seen an apple. We place in front of him several kinds of fruit including a red apple. To make things simple, the apple is the only red fruit in the group. If we ask him to choose the red apple, he will be able to point to it without hesitation. Next, we ask him to tell us whether the apple is large or small. Since he has never seen an apple before, he will be unable to say whether the apple in front of him is large or small.

This experiment makes it clear that as long as a person knows the meaning of the adjective *red*, he can judge immediately whether or not an object before him is red. He needs no more detailed knowledge or information about it. But, in order to be able to call a certain object large, he will actually have to know more about it and the category to which it belongs.

Next let us suppose our subject has never seen an elephant. If we take him to a zoo and show him an elephant, he will probably say in amazement, "Isn't it large!" Although he has never seen an elephant before, he can still apply the adjective *large*. Recall that this same person was unable to answer the question, "Is this apple large or small?" about the first apple he had ever seen. How do we account for this?

Large in the phrase *a large apple* usually means "large for an apple." What counts is the size of a given sample within the framework of a specific species called "apple." In other words, one normally knows from experience how large an average apple is and can judge the size of the apple in question, using this knowledge as a measure. Thus, someone who sees an apple for the first time has no way of determining whether it is large or small.

But then, why is it that the person seeing an elephant for the first time at the zoo goes home saying, "I saw a large elephant"? In this case, his statement may be interpreted to mean that the elephant is larger than all the *other* animals he has seen. What he means is not "large for an elephant," but "large for an animal."

It becomes clear from the two different uses of the adjective *large*, with reference to an apple and an elephant, that in order to be able to designate something as *large*, one needs some sort of criterion. Only when measured against a given norm can something be judged large or small. For this reason, such adjectives as *large* and *small* are called relative adjectives in linguistics.

In contrast, *akai* 'red' is an example of an absolute adjective. Those who have learned the range of the color spectrum called *akai* 'red' in Japanese will be able to recognize immediately all the red objects they encounter, whether or not they have seen them before.[1] They can state without hesitation that Japanese mailboxes, fire engines, and the circle in the middle of the Japanese flag are all red. In other words, *red* may be said to refer to a property rooted or anchored in individual objects, but *long* and *large* refer to relationships between objects and do not have roots in an individual object per se.

Comparatives

In spite of all this, when we say a certain item is *long-short* or *large-small*, not even linguists have given much thought to the distinction between these adjectives and others like *red* and *round*. One reason is that both groups are, at least superficially, quite similar in function. In fact, both groups of adjectives have been classified together in most grammars simply as "qualitative adjectives"; they were given the same treatment in classical logic. But as is already clear from the explanation above, when one says an object is *large* or *long*, one is unconsciously comparing it with other objects of the same type. In this sense, *large* and *long* are structurally different from *red*.

Now I would like to consider just what kinds of covert measures, or hidden criteria, for comparison are actually operative in our use of these adjectives.

The adjectives *large* and *long* are sometimes used in explicit comparison. One can say, for example, "A is larger than B," or one can hold two articles before one's eyes and say, "This is longer." In such cases, it is obvious to everyone that the speaker is comparing two objects. On the other hand, the statement "Isn't it large!" uttered by someone looking at an elephant is in itself already a comparative sentence. This may not be immediately clear to everyone because the norm for comparison is not verbalized. Sentences such as *A is large* (or *small*) and *B is long* (or *short*) should therefore be called "covert comparatives."

In contrast, I call such sentences as *A is larger than B*, which are specified as comparative sentences in grammar, "overt comparatives." In this type of comparison, B is the measure while A is called a specimen, in the sense that it is the object being compared. Even in overt comparatives, however, measures are not always stated. In the sentence *Mt. Fuji is the highest mountain in Japan*, the measure is "all the other mountains in Japan," which is deleted. On the contrary, in *This apple is large*, there is a specimen (*this apple*), but no apparent measure. It is therefore necessary to make a distinction between measures which do not have to be mentioned because they are tacitly understood by everyone and latent measures, of which even the speakers themselves are unaware.

(1) The Specific Norm. The most commonly used covert norm is the one called "the specific norm." As in the example of the apple above, when we say something is large or small, we have in mind the general average size of the species represented by the thing in question. Using that as a norm, we measure the particular specimen in front of us. If the apple in question is the size of an egg, most people will say it is small. If, however, one sees an apple the size of a prize watermelon at a fair, one will definitely call it large. These judgments of course cannot be absolute. Depending on people's experience and the extent of their knowledge,

60

the "average" size of an apple may vary. Furthermore, most speakers do not realize that they are making a kind of subconscious comparison. Precisely for this reason, arguments over whether a certain object is large or small often cannot be settled.

The specific norm, as one can see, varies with each species. Therefore even a slightly odd sentence like "A long pencil, no matter how long, is shorter than the shortest ski" can crop up. When one judges something, one sometimes uses the expression "considering the fact that" to imply what species he has in mind. For example, with reference to a medium-sized watermelon grown in an amateur vegetable garden, one might say, "This watermelon is large, considering the fact that it was grown by an amateur." But even in this case, the measure itself is covert just as in the other examples.

(2)   The Proportion Norm. Anyone who has studied English as a foreign language should remember the difficulty he had in trying to learn the minute differences in usage between synonyms. One such confusing pair of synonyms is *high* and *tall*.

When referring to a person, the normal usage is to say "He is tall" or "He is a tall man." *High* is not used in such a case. Both *high* and *tall* may be used to describe such things as buildings and trees. One may feel that it is possible to describe the difference between these two adjectives. But if one is asked to do so, the difficulty becomes apparent. The difference, in my view, can be efficiently explained as follows. *High* is an adjective focusing on the distance from the ground to the top of the object in question or to the object itself. *High* is used in this way about buildings and trees. Since this adjective only concerns the spatial distance between a

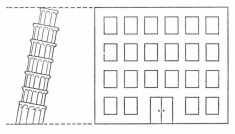

Figure 5

certain object and the ground, it may also be used with regard to things floating in the air like clouds.

On the other hand, *tall* does not concern the mere distance (or height) from the ground to a certain object; rather it is concerned with the proportion of height to width. Expressions such as *a tall tree* or *a tall tower* imply that the height of the object in question is disproportionately greater than its width (figure 5). This explains why, with respect to a person, one must use *tall* to express one's general impression of physique. Of two people of the same height, the thinner one is more likely to be described as *tall*.

Such words as *tall*, which measures a property of a certain object by using another characteristic of the same object as a covert norm, may be called adjectives based on proportion norms. The Japanese word *hosonagai* 'slender' is an adjective of this type. The word which corresponds to *tall* in Japanese is probably *hyoronagai*, which, like *tall*, can be used only for something that is normally vertical.

(3) The Expectation Norm. If a young nephew or someone related to us comes to visit us after a long while, we often say something like "Aren't you a tall boy now! I wouldn't have recognized you if I had met you somewhere

else." To this the child might reply bashfully, "But, Uncle, I am smaller than average in my class." Here, the child is comparing himself with his classmates, using the specific norm. On the other hand, the uncle is unconsciously comparing his nephew as he now sees him with his memory of the child's size at the time of their last meeting (figure 6). The uncle had retained a certain image of the child's height in mind, but his nephew has grown considerably in the meantime, and the uncle expresses his surprise with "Aren't you a tall boy now!" Thus, when an individual applies a measure which he has developed in his mind, we call it the expectation norm.

A child asks his parents for an allowance and receives one thousand yen. He complains, saying it is too little, to which the parents angrily reply, "It might be too much, but can't be too little." To the parents, who are using the specific norm, it is too much "for a child's allowance," while to the child, who is judging by the expectation norm, the same allowance seems too little. If the child then says, "But

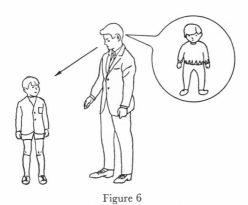

Figure 6

my friend Tarō gets a much bigger allowance," he is making an overt comparison rather than a covert one.

(4) The Utility Norm. Another one of the covert norms is used when one makes a judgment from the standpoint of whether a given object is useful for a certain purpose.

Let us now consider the Japanese adjectives *semai* 'limited in space, narrow' and *hiroi* 'roomy, spacious, wide,' which we use in reference to such things as rooms. At first, expressions like *semai heya* ' a room limited in space' and *hiroi heya* 'a spacious room' may seem to be based on specific norms. But how is it, then, that we also say *ōkī heya* 'a large room' and *chīsai heya* 'a small room'? If we consider this further, it becomes clear that whether a room is *semai* or *hiroi* is determined by how many people are using it and for what purpose. Even a large twenty-mat room (15 by 24 feet) would become inadequately *semai* if a banquet for three hundred guests were to take place there, whereas a ten-mat room (12 by 15 feet) might be too *hiroi* for just one person to sleep in comfortably.

Whether an entryway is *semai* 'narrow' or *hiroi* 'wide,' depends on the number of people going through it at one time. Of course, an entryway barely wide enough for one person is always *semai*, but even this description is based on the degree of usefulness of the entrance for the purpose of walking through it.

Thus, adjectives based on utility norms do not describe properties of things and objects per se; instead, they only express how appropriate or useful they are for a particular purpose. Nevertheless, we normally and incorrectly assume that when we say *semai heya* 'a room limited in space' or *hiroi iriguchi* 'a wide entryway,' these expressions describe

64

properties of the objects in the same way that expressions such as *akarui heya* 'a light room' or *rippa na iriguchi* 'a grand entryway' do.

Semai signifies an object being not sufficiently wide or spacious enough for a particular activity. It is, however, neutral with respect to the question of whether that is desirable or undesirable. In other words, something being *semai* could be either convenient or inconvenient. The entrance to a castle, for example, might purposely be made *semai* to make it easier to repulse enemy attacks, and some people might feel more at home in a *semai heya* 'a room limited in area.'

But there are many Japanese expressions based on the utility norm that are definitely committed to a positive or negative evaluation. Suppose a mother has just bought her young son a school uniform that is on the large side, hoping he can wear it for many months to come. The son may complain to the mother, saying, "This uniform is *dabudabu* 'too loose.'" She may reply, "But it is *yuttari* 'not too tight.' You'll feel comfortable in it." Both *dabudabu* and *yuttari* share the same objective judgment about the uniform being too large, but whereas *dabudabu* is based on a negative evaluation of the excessive size as something undesirable, *yuttari* treats the same state as desirable. In Japanese, we also have expressions like *tsuntsuruten* 'too short,' *suntarazu* 'not long enough,' and *kitsui* 'tight' to refer to clothing size which is insufficient in some respect. All of these are derogatory expressions based on a negative evalution of a deficiency along one dimension or another.

Among the Japanese words to describe clothes sizes, there are other common expressions based on the utility norm such

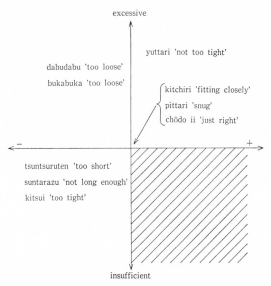

Figure 7

as *pittari* 'snug' and *chōdo ii* 'just right.' These two terms express one's judgment that a certain piece of clothing is neither too large nor too small, but just the right size for the wearer.

If, from the standpoint above, these clothes-related words based on utility norms are summarized as in figure 7, an interesting fact becomes apparent: not one word in this category can denote a deficiency in size and still have a positive connotation. This is probably to be expected, considering the nature of clothing.

Adjectives like *semai* 'narrow, limited in area' are almost always used only from the standpoint of the utility norm. The utility norm itself, however, may be applied to many other adjectives. For example, although the use of *ōkī* 'large,

66

big' is based on the specific norm when reference is to the objective size of something, and on the expectation norm when reference is to subjective individual judgments, its use can be based on the utility norm as well. The utility norm is operative in a statement such as "I need an *ōkī* 'large' stone for my pickle tub."† Adjectives such as *ōkī* which refer to various dimensions are often used with an implied utility norm.

(5) The Anthropomorphic Norm. Swiss linguist Ernst Leisi first pointed out the four kinds of covert criteria for comparison discussed above.[2] Since the publication of his study in 1953, many scholars have conducted research directed at discovering new criteria. Although to date I have not heard of any other discoveries, I myself once published an article introducing one possible new criterion, to be called "the anthropomorphic norm."[3]

We often make such statements as *The elephant has a long 'hana'* 'nose, trunk' and *The giraffe has a long neck*. What norm do we have in mind when we say that the elephant's *hana* is long?

To begin with, the sentence *The elephant has a long 'hana'* may be regarded as a concrete expression in everyday language of what is called "a universal proposition" in logic. This sentence may therefore be rephrased as follows: "If a certain object is an elephant, and has something called a *hana*, then that *hana* is always long." In simpler terms, it may be paraphrased as "The trunk of every elephant is long." It is easy to make any number of sentences of this sort by choosing an animal having a certain salient physical feature:

†Japanese pickles are made in a tub with a heavy weight on top for pressure.

The giraffe has a long neck.
The pig has a short tail.
The crane has a long neck.

Now let us consider what norm is behind *long* and *short* in the sentences above. First of all, it is obvious that the specific norm is not operative here. As explained earlier, the specific norm underlies the exclamation "Isn't this a large apple!" at the sight of an apple the size of a watermelon displayed at a country fair. The exclamation means that the particular apple being referred to is large, in the sense that it is larger than an average apple. We use the specific norm, when we make a judgment about a specimen, a particular sample of a species. It is operative in what is known in logic as a "particular proposition." Therefore, the specific norm which produces particular propositions, and a sentence like *The elephant has a long 'hana,'* which is characterized as a universal proposition, are mutually exclusive in nature. Those who would insist that the specific norm is operative in the sentence about the elephant's nose must explain its use by regarding all animals (or all mammals), that is, the larger group of which the elephant is a member, as one species. *The elephant has a long 'hana'* has the sense that a particular member of the animal kingdom (the elephant) has a *hana* which is longer than the average length *hana* of the other members.

The trouble with this interpretation is that animals, even if we limit ourselves only to mammals, represent a tremendous variety, which makes it nearly impossible for us to figure out the average length of an animal's *hana*. If not impossible, at least we must admit that no one has at his disposal such a mental measure as "the average length of an animal's *hana*"—a handy yardstick, so to speak, which could be used readily to determine whether a given *hana* is long or short.

Can we, then, interpret the elephant sentence as a judgment based on the proportion norm? This at first seems like a more appropriate interpretation. The proportion norm, as explained earlier, is a norm which is applied when one dimension of an object is measured against another dimension of the same object. If we look at the trunk of an elephant in this way, its length is indeed remarkable in comparison with its width (or diameter). It therefore seems quite possible that the proportion norm applies in this case. However, this explanation is also inadequate.

Suppose we compare the legs of a crane with those of a sparrow. No one would deny that the former are long, and many would call the latter short. In any case, the legs of a sparrow are not a conspicuous feature of the bird. But when we focus our attention on the legs themselves and examine the proportion of their length to their width, we discover that they are really quite slender. That is to say, proportionally speaking, the legs of a sparrow are much greater in length than in width. Even so, we normally do not call them long. From this example, we conclude that when we say "long legs" or "a long *hana*" with reference to a certain animal having a salient physical feature, we are not concerned with the shape of that part alone, but rather with some sort of proportional ratio between the part in question and the size of the whole body.

Let us now go back to the elephant. The elephant is the largest animal on land. If it had a *hana* neither too long nor too short but just right for an animal of that size, what

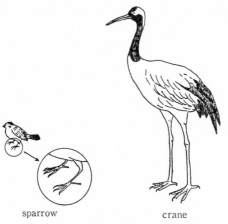

sparrow   crane

Figure 8

length would it be? What we consider "the right length" for an elephant's *hana* is the criterion we must have in our minds, the norm which makes us say "The elephant has a long *hana*" at the sight of an actual elephant trunk. The crucial element here is obviously the proportional ratio between the *hana* and the whole body which would seem harmonious to us as humans, and not the ratio between the length and the width of the *hana* itself.

When we say *long, short, thick, thin*, etc., with reference to conspicuous physical features of various animals, the crucial norm is the degree of proportion between the part of the body in question and the whole of the body. If that is the case, what determines our ideas of basic harmonious proportions between a particular part of an animal and its whole body? In my opinion, the sense of proportion derived from the human body is applied as a measure (sometimes used expansively and figuratively) when we look at other animals.

70

In support of this argument, I cite the fact that universal propositions such as *The elephant has a long 'hana'* cannot generally be made with reference to parts of the human body. *Man has long arms* is an odd sentence. In fact, such a sentence never occurs. But that is not because man has short arms, for *Man has short arms* sounds equally odd. *The elephant has a short 'hana'* is odd because it is contrary to fact, but the oddness of the universal propositions stated above about man's arms cannot be due to their being contrary to fact.

But sentences about individuals such as *This person has long arms* and *Tarō has short arms* and sentences about specific groups of people such as *The Japanese have short legs* do not sound odd at all. This makes it clear that particular propositions about humans are possible while universal ones are not. Needless to say, in particular propositions, specific norms determine the use of *long* and *short*. If the subject is a boy named Tarō, the specific norm is the Japanese in general; if the subject is the Japanese people, mankind is the implied specific norm.

Because the proportions between the human body and its individual parts are employed as a measure to determine the degree of harmony in the appearance of animals, statements such as *Man has long* (or *short*) *arms* which refer directly to this measure, that is, to the model of harmonious proportion, are meaningless. Instead, we use this standard to describe the characteristics of other animals. We do not say *The cat has a short* (or *long*) *neck* because the ratio of the cat's neck to its body falls well within the boundary of our sense of harmony. On the contrary, the trunk of an elephant or the neck of a giraffe strikes us as disproportionate and unbalanced.

71

Naturally, people today are not very surprised at the sight of elephants or giraffes. They have been acquainted with them since childhood through drawings and photographs and have sometimes even seen them in real life. Even so, each of us must have been amazed when we saw the strange figures of elephants or giraffes for the first time, in pictures or in reality. Such sentences as *The elephant has a long 'hana'* are man's verbal expression of surprise at these strange figures, and the sense of proportion used as the norm by which to judge them as abnormal seems ultimately to derive from the proportions between the human body and its parts.

There is an ancient Greek adage that man is the measure of everything, and the anthropomorphic norm is perfect proof of this saying. Indeed, the way we organize the surrounding world through language is always anthropocentric, and man is always taken as the norm.

4. Meanings and Definitions

Sound and Meaning

A word, no matter what language it may belong to, and no matter what kind of word it may be, always consists of two parts. First, it has its sound, or phonological shape, which might be called its external form. Second, it has its content, commonly known as meaning. A word, therefore, combines a specific phonological shape and a fixed meaning. In linguistics, which is supposed to be the science of language, however, the study of word meaning lags far behind the study of sound, which has had a long history and has accordingly made tremendous progress.

In both historical comparative linguistics, which came into being in eighteenth-century Europe and reached its peak in the following century, and in descriptive structural linguistics, which made great strides in the first half of the twentieth century, research centered around the phonological side of language. This trend was especially evident in American linguistics during the first half of this century, when the emphasis was heavily scientific and behavioristic. The study of word meaning, as well as of meaning itself, an important component of language, was treated as a nonlinguistic mental phenomenon and was almost excluded from the linguistic world.

The reason for this imbalance is simple. Sound is a physical phenomenon and clearly definable. Even sounds from the remote past have been preserved in writing in some cases, though imperfectly. The study of sound, therefore, did not have to begin with the definition of speech sounds. Unlike the study of meaning, it was blessed with a self-evident measurable phenomenon for research from the start.

Word meaning, the content part of language, is mainly concerned with the mental activities of man; it offers nothing concrete for objective study and has, therefore, been considered too elusive for research. Much argument has taken place on the issue of the nature of linguistic meaning, and a number of definitions have been attempted, but no conclusive answer has been forthcoming even to this day. As a result, research in this area has remained sporadic and limited in scope in comparison to other areas of linguistic study.

In the second half of the twentieth century, however, linguistics has advanced by leaps and bounds. Energetic efforts are being made to explain meaning as a grammatical fact by expanding the framework of grammatical theory. There is little doubt, however, that in the extremely complicated area of linguistic meaning, questions that await elucidation far outweigh those that have already been explained.

Where Dictionaries Fail

While linguists have groped in the dark for solutions to the problem of meaning, there has been a field which of necessity treats the meanings of words as something clear, as if they could be easily explained. This is the field of dictionary making.

One of the important functions of a dictionary is to explain to people words whose meanings they do not know. Certainly, when people have to find the meaning of a word for themselves or explain its meaning to others, the best source of information is a dictionary.

Thus, a look at the treatment of meanings of words in dictionaries, instead of comparing meaning in the light of various linguistic theories, might bring about unexpectedly interesting results. It may be feasible to explore the question of meaning via the exit, as it were, rather than via the entrance. One might in this way find clues to linguistic meaning. After all, whether or not dictionary editors successfully deal with meaning, they are well-known specialists of particular languages and are far from being amateurs in the field of language.

With this possibility in mind, I once examined dictionaries of different languages. Previously, when I used dictionaries for no other purpose than to learn the meaning of a word, I sometimes found satisfactory answers, but more than once I was annoyed by what dictionary editors felt should pass as a definition.

Then when I examined the content of each definition on the tacit assumption that a dictionary, however imperfectly, explains the meanings of words, I began to notice some extremely interesting points. The most important discovery for me was that all dictionary editors fail to distinguish between the "meaning" and the "definition" of a word, thereby frequently falling into unnecessary difficulties.[1]

In the following sections, I will first of all dispose of a few peripheral problems common to all dictionaries. After that, I will explore the broader issues: why it is necessary to distinguish the "meaning" of a word from its "definition," and how this distinction helps clarify what has been heretofore vaguely termed as linguistic meaning.

Defining *Ishi*

First, as I explained in some detail in chapter one with reference to the structures of *break* and *drink*, defining a word by the substitution of another word that only partially corresponds in usage has the significant shortcoming of being unable to indicate the full meaning of the original word properly. Even if, for example, an English-Japanese dictionary tries to explain *break* by listing such Japanese words as *kowasu, waru, kiru,* and *oru,* the dictionary user will still fail to grasp the exact content of *break* unless he is consciously aware of the content of the Japanese verbs themselves.

The same problem arises in Japanese-language dictionaries. In one dictionary, *sūhai suru* 'to worship' is defined as *agame uyamau* 'to revere and venerate.' In this case, word A has merely been replaced by words B and C; this does not really explain the meaning of A. With this substitution method, one can walk around the problem of "meaning" for a while. But the fact that one has only temporarily avoided direct confrontation with the issue is evident, since the meanings of the words given in the definition, i.e., *agame uyamau*, must eventually be explained. It follows that the only effective way to get a true picture of how word meanings are explained in a dictionary is to examine cases where this evasive substitution method no longer works, cases where dictionary editors are cornered, as it were, and cannot fall back on substitution.

In light of this, let us see how one of the best known Japanese dictionaries defines the word *ishi* 'stone': "a small piece of matter which is harder than soil or wood, heavier than water, larger than a grain of sand *(suna)* and smaller than a large rock *(iwa)*."[2] It is fortunate that few people are likely to look up this word. The inadequacy of the definition is so evident. Pieces of iron, lead, glass, or even bone may be called *ishi* according to this definition.

What is worse, however, is that although I was using the dictionary to find the meaning of *ishi*, I encountered in its definition such other words as *suna* and *iwa*, and these other words actually cannot be explained without using the word *ishi*. The same dictionary defines *suna* as "very fine grains of *ishi*," and *iwa* as "a large *ishi*." This is indeed a vicious circle: if a person does not know what the word *ishi* means before he looks it up, he cannot understand the meaning of the definition!

Let me cite another example. If I look up the adjective *itai* 'to be painful,' I find the explanation *itami o kanjiru* 'to feel a pain.' But if I look up the noun *itami* 'a pain,' it is explained as *itamu koto; sono jōtai* 'the state of something being painful.' The verb *itamu*, in turn, is defined as *(nikutai ni) itami o kanzuru* 'to feel a (physical) pain,' thus sending one right back to the starting point.

In the case of *ishi*, as well as *itai*, the dictionary is obviously guilty of circular definition. I should point out here, however, that this situation is not limited to dictionaries edited in Japan; those of other countries are not much different.

For example, the *Concise Oxford Dictionary* defines *pain* as "n. Suffering, distress of body or mind." But the definition of *suffer*, "v.t. & i. Undergo, experience, be subject to (pain, loss . . .)," includes the original word, *pain*. How did this all come about?

Explanations of the meanings of such self-evident words as *ishi*, *itai*, and *nomu* (see pages 17–19) are full of flaws in any dictionary. I will tentatively call these "basic words" because their meanings cannot be explained by citing or listing easier words in their place.

The Meanings of Words

Let us now consider how we learned these so-called basic words. The first thing they have in common is that we learned them quite unconsciously. In every language, children acquire basic words effortlessly while living through everyday situations. In this way they learn phonological shapes of words and their meanings together as a harmonious whole. Children do not have to ask the meanings of basic words.

When learning more difficult words, such as antiquated words, loanwords, and technical terms, however, we typically go through the following process. First, we hear a word spoken or see it in print, and then ask someone what it means. Or we may first see an object and then ask someone what it is called.

With basic words, there is no such separation of sound and content. Sound and content always go together as a set, neither one preceding the other. It makes no sense, therefore, to ask self-explanatory questions such as "What is *ishi*?" and

"What does *itai* mean?" Because their meanings are empirically so clear, they need not be explained with other words.

A basic vocabulary is thus shared by virtually everyone who belongs to the same language community. Each person can use it effortlessly. Does this mean that everyone understands all basic words in exactly the same fashion? Not really, since each person has had a different experience with any given word.

Consider the word *dog*. The word *dog* evokes very different images in the minds of those who have been bitten by dogs and those who have not. Dog lovers can distinguish different kinds of dogs and point out their respective characteristics, while people who are not interested in dogs cannot. But this does not keep anyone from understanding and using the word *dog*. With this in mind, I feel that the meaning of a word should be as follows: the sum total of all the individual experience and knowledge we have in connection with a certain phonological shape.

If the "meaning" of a word is defined in this way, two characteristics may be said to be part of meaning: (1) the meaning of a word varies greatly from individual to individual; (2) the meaning of a word cannot be transmitted by using other words. These points need further explanation.

As mentioned above, people who like dogs and those who do not are widely separated in terms of accumulated experience and knowledge concerning dogs. Nevertheless, both groups know the meaning of the word *dog*. Of course, the meaning of a word is known to vary with the user. But what varies from individual to individual has usually been regarded as the peripheral or nonessential elements of lin-

Figure 3

The famous story about a group of
blind men who tried to determine
what an elephant was like by feeling
it with their hands demonstrates very
clearly how people's interpretations
of the same object, and therefore of
the same word, can differ from one
another.

guistic meaning known as connotative, or emotive, meaning.
The central core of meaning, usually known as denotative
meaning, has been thought of as a socially stable item shared
by all with only minor variations from individual to individual. Traditional studies have been devoted to discovering
this common denominator and generalizing it.

In my opinion, it is both unnecessary and impossible to
make a distinction between connotative and denotative
meaning. It is of course natural that, in the case of a word
like *dog* referring to a common domestic animal, people
share a large part of the meaning of the word. But as soon as
we replace *dog* by *wolf*, it immediately becomes evident how

different each person's understanding of the same word can be. Children have only a limited knowledge about wolves through fairy tales and children's stories such as *Little Red Riding Hood*. Hunters are fully familiar with the looks, tracks, feces, routes, and habits of wolves. Zoologists not only know all species of wolves and their worldwide distribution, but also have a taxonomic knowledge of their anatomy. In other words, the understanding of the same word *wolf* varies greatly across these three groups. Other groups would, of course, interpret the term in yet other ways. To me this signifies that the traditional view—that part of the meaning of a word which is shared by everyone is its social meaning— is an empty fiction with hardly any basis in fact.

Let me illustrate my point using Japanese examples. For most Japanese city dwellers today, words such as *konnyaku* 'devil's tongue, a jellylike food made from the starch of of devil's tongue,' *tabako* 'tobacco, cigarette,' and *wata* 'cotton' probably signify only products made from these plants. To their minds, *konnyaku* is an ingredient used in Japanese cuisine; *tabako* is a substance to be chopped up, wrapped in paper, and sold by the pack; *wata* refers to absorbent cotton balls or, possibly, the fluffy material inside a quilted kimono. Urban residents going to the country are unable to identify the plants which yield the materials for these products. Very few people these days know that *konnyaku* comes from the bulbous root of a plant similar to the taro. Farmers and city dwellers actually have very little in common in terms of their knowledge of and experience with these words. If the shared meaning of a word truly constituted its social, denotative meaning, then *konnyaku*, strangely enough, would have to mean a rectangular chunk of jelly made from the starch of devil's tongue. Reference to the plant itself would be a function of the connotative, emotive meaning of the word!

In order to avoid such a strange outcome, we may define the meaning of a word as the sum total of an individual's knowledge and experience connected with its phonological form. This will more accurately reflect linguistic reality.

Now let me turn to the second point, that the meaning of a word cannot be transmitted with words.

If we define the meaning of a word as above, it is only natural that we cannot transmit it to others merely by using other words (although people can, of course, talk about their experiences to others). For example, it is impossible for us to convey the taste of chocolate to someone who has never eaten chocolate merely by describing its taste. That is why I say the meaning of a word is verbally intransmissible.

But even though we may accept the new definition of the meaning of a word, we do sometimes learn new words from others or teach words to them, which proves that words are socially transmissible. How do we reconcile this undeniable fact with the intransmissibility of meaning?

Definitions

In my opinion, when we teach words to others, we teach "definitions" of words, not "meanings." The "definition" (there are various kinds, which I will explain later) of a word is transmissible. Let me clarify this point with an example.

The word *shibui* 'astringent' is defined in the Japanese dictionary cited earlier as follows: "a stinging and numbing sensation felt on the tongue when eating a *shibugaki* 'astringent persimmon' and the like." This explanation says nothing about what *shibui* 'astringent' or *shibusa* 'astringent quality' means. What is mentioned is how the feeling of *shibui*, as known to the dictionary editors, may be attained by the reader; it is, as it were, a set of directions on how to reach a certain destination. Things beyond that point are all left to the unverifiable, although intuitively plausible, assumption that all people can obtain identical (or similar) experiences under identical (or similar) conditions. It essentially says the following: "Do not merely look at, but eat, an unripe green persimmon instead of a ripe red one. The sensation you experience on your tongue is the sensation called *shibusa* in Japanese."

In fact, the social learning of a word always takes place exactly in this manner. This is what I call the "definition" of a word. To "define" is to delimit the range within which a word is applicable, that is, to clarify the boundaries within which a word may be used appropriately.

The most basic type of definition is to point to something and say, "This is such-and-such." This is usually called definition by designation. It is the simplest kind of definition but it also has various shortcomings. For one thing, it requires that the object in question be present. More importantly, it is not always clear to the addressee what part of the object the speaker is focusing on as he speaks.

Suppose we show an infant a ball and say, "This is a ball." The little child might assume that *ball* means "anything spherical." As a result, he might start producing the word *ball* at the sight of any spherical object, even watermelons and peas. His parents will probably laugh and correct him. The child learns that the word *ball* cannot be used for peas or watermelons. As he continues using the word *ball* with different objects, sometimes eliciting praise, sometimes laughter, he gradually realizes that *ball* may be applied only to a certain type of object which satisfies certain conditions.

Instead of pointing to an object, we sometimes try to teach someone a word by means of other words. This is essentially an alternative to repeating definitions by designation many times, under many different circumstances. In other words, what we do in such cases is to set limits and spell out the conditions regulating the use of a word so that the other person may acquire the same experience that we have regarding a certain word. Therefore, the definition of a word through the medium of other words may take an infinite variety of forms, depending on the differences in experience between the speaker and the addressee, as well as on the purpose for which the word is being defined.

For example, suppose we are teaching the word *lion* to a child who does not know what a lion is. If he already knows what a cat is, we can narrow the boundaries of the object considerably by describing a lion as a big cat. But even then the child will be unable to distinguish a lion from a tiger or a leopard. We will have to describe the animal in more detail. But no matter how detailed the description, it can never be complete in the absolute sense of the word.

In the final analysis, whether a certain verbal definition of a word is correct or sufficient depends upon whether the person giving the definition succeeds in providing the addressee with an understanding of the term adequate to their mutual purpose. We must realize that there can be no such thing as a flawless definition which can satisfy everyone, everywhere, at all times.

No Need to Define *Ishi*

Let us now go back to the question we posed earlier in this chapter. How are the meanings of words treated in dictionaries? If we recognize the impossibility of transmitting the "meaning" of a word using other words, we must also admit that the only possible role of a dictionary is to "define" words. From this viewpoint, let us consider once again the examples of *ishi* 'stone' and *itai* 'painful.' In both cases, the dictionary explanations were circular definitions, which did not bring us closer to understanding. There is, however, a distinct difference between the two.

The attempt to describe *ishi* as "larger than *suna* 'a grain of sand,' smaller than *iwa* 'a good-sized rock,' harder than soil, heavier than water . . ." is correct in the sense that the description, however imperfect, is oriented toward a definition. The problem comes in the use, within the definition, of such words as *iwa* and *suna* which in turn cannot be defined without using the word *ishi*.

In my view, however, there is absolutely no need to define *ishi* in a Japanese dictionary. A definition after all is an attempt to lead the addressee (or the reader) into attaining the closest possible approximation of the experience which the speaker (or the writer) has in connection with a certain word. It therefore makes no sense to try to define *ishi* for Japanese people, who already have an empirical knowledge of what an *ishi* is. It is like trying to tell someone who has already reached the top of Mt. Fuji how to climb it.

The inadequacy of describing *itai* 'painful' as *itami o kanzuru koto* 'to feel a pain' is different in nature. Such a description is completely meaningless; it is a tautology. If

85

one were to define *itai*, however meaningless and imperfect such an attempt might be, it would be better to give the reader a guide to achieving the sensation. One might say, for example, "what one feels when pricked with a needle" or "the sensation one has when one breaks a leg." In this sense, the dictionary definition of *shibui* 'astringent' as "a stinging sensation felt on the tongue when eating a *shibu-gaki* 'astringent persimmon' " is fairly satisfactory, although *astringent persimmon* should be replaced by *unripe persimmon* to avoid a tautology.

Verbs and Adjectives versus Nouns

As a result of defining the terms "meaning" and "definition" as above, something of which I was formerly only vaguely aware has become very clear. Not only are verbs and adjectives easier to define than nouns, but they can also be defined with more universality. Things and objects which are represented by nonderivative nouns have, in most cases, an almost infinite number of aspects. Even one particular plant, for example, may require all kinds of information. What are its taxonomical properties and position, as well as its shape and distribution? Is it poisonous or not? If edible, what part of it should be cooked and in what way? How much does it cost? There are many ways in which the plant affects one's life, and all these factors may be included in the definition. A universal definition, satisfactory to everyone, would seem to be nearly an impossibility.

Whether or not one can make a distinction between linguistic knowledge and factual knowledge has become an issue in linguistic study today. In my opinion, such a distinction cannot be made, at least when dealing with non-derivative nouns. One must accept that the definitions of words themselves are directly dependent on the knowledge and the experience of the people who use them, and that these factors are infinitely varied and renewable.

In contrast, verbs can be defined much more objectively. This is attested by the examples given in chapter one, but here I will add one more example for further illustration. In English, there is a basic verb *wear*. If one describes its uses in the traditional English-Japanese dictionary fashion, one has to list all kinds of Japanese verbs—*kaburu* for hats, *kiru* for suits and jackets, *haku* for shoes, *kakeru* for eyeglasses, *hameru* for rings, (*tokei o*) *suru* for wristwatches, *tsukeru* for underwear, and so on. *Wear* in *He wears his hair long* and *She wears her hair waved* corresponds to *nobashite-iru* and *kakete-iru*, respectively. In English, the same verb is also used in such expressions as *wear a smile*, *wear a sour look*, and *wear perfume*; corresponding expressions in Japanese require a different verb in each case: *ukaberu*, (*shikametsura o*) *suru*, and *tsukeru*, respectively. Thus, if we follow the practice of listing corresponding words in Japanese, we need more than ten different verbs to account for all the uses of *wear*. Even then, it is possible that these verbs will not exactly cover all the areas of meaning represented by *wear*.

I tried, therefore, to discover a viewpoint from which to summarize all the uses of *wear*. Finally, I realized that they all have one element in common, that is, the presence of something on the surface of the human body. Wearing clothing, rings, and perfume can all be interpreted in this way. So can wearing hair, smiles, and facial expressions. Furthermore, since expressions like *a smile* and *his hair* fall under the same grammatical category as other expressions like *a hat* and *a ring*, it is not unnatural for all of them to be used as the object of the same verb *wear*, however unnatural it might seem to Japanese speakers.

This explanation, however, does not solve all the problems. We can say *He wears his hair long* and *She wears her hair waved*, but not **He wears his hair black*.[3] Moreover, *wear* cannot take as its object things like moles, although they are located on the surface of the body. After thinking the matter over, I discovered the need to add one more condition: temporary selection. That is to say, one voluntarily selects something to wear for a limited period of time.

This definition of *wear* covers all the uses of the verb in a very abstract and objective way, completely unhindered by individual concrete objects and states. It is not only hats and clothes that one voluntarily chooses to wear. Wearing one's hair long or wearing a beard is also a voluntary act. A person can have his long hair cut short or shave off his beard when tired of it. On the other hand, moles and black hair are not due to voluntary choice, nor are they temporary. This explains why we cannot use *wear* with reference to these things.

Neither British and American dictionaries nor Japanese dictionaries give us such abstract definitions, but since "to choose something voluntarily and attach it temporarily to the surface of one's body" includes almost all the correct uses of *wear*, it may be called a fairly absolute definition.

Prepositions, which express relations between things, can also be defined objectively. In light of this, it is interesting to note that research in meaning in the area of verbs, adjectives, and prepositions is relatively advanced in many languages, but little work has been done in the area of nouns, with the exception of kinship terms and the like, which in themselves contain structural relationships. This may be due to the fact that nouns represent concrete things, which are intrinsically difficult to define because they are multifaceted, with different values attached to them by different individuals. Some dictionaries make use of illustrations and photographs to describe words pertaining to concrete objects. Some people feel uncomfortable with this procedure, for they feel that pictures cannot be "meanings." Whether or not they are, in fact, "meanings," we may still consider illustrative material very effective and accurate "definitions" of a large number of terms.

In chapter one, I suggested that dictionaries elucidate the necessary and sufficient conditions regulating the use of each word so that its meaning might be more tightly presented, which in turn would increase the effectiveness of the dictionaries. Actually that suggestion does not apply to most nouns, since objects cannot be completely pinned down by words.

5. Values Which Give Meaning to Facts

Are the Japanese Cruel?

The occupation forces, which moved into Japan right after its defeat in World War II, controlled the mass media and incessantly disseminated information as to what atrocities the Japanese armed forces had committed and what an incomparably cruel nation the Japanese were. At the same time, Japan's wartime leaders were being tried as "war criminals" by the Allied Forces at the military tribunal in Ichigaya, Tokyo. In those days, determined to renew my study of English, I often listened to broadcasts of the war crimes trials, using them as instructional materials for living English. I still vividly remember that I learned such words as *atrocity* and *cruelty* from those broadcasts.

It was not necessarily just the victorious occupation forces who made a big issue of this supposed cruelty. The Japanese themselves, under the influence of slogans such as *Ichioku Sō Zange* 'Time of Repentance for All the Hundred Million Japanese,' were exposing one inhuman act after another they had committed, such as the "Bataan Death March" and the "Nanking Massacre."

In those days, just across the street from my house in Tokyo, a naval attaché to the British Embassy moved in with his family. One day, I heard some puppies yelping outside my gate. Since I am a dog lover, I rushed to the scene. Someone had obviously abandoned a litter of puppies; four mongrels about a month old were whining in the gutter by the gate. I wondered what to do. It was a time of miserable food shortages and keeping one dog was difficult enough, four being out of the question. Soon the puppies, for some reason, crawled under the concrete cover of the gutter and started crying.

First, I thought to myself, they had to be fed, so I went for a broom and with it began pulling them from under the cover. At that moment, I heard a loud yell above me. I looked up in consternation and saw the naval attaché's wife apparently furious and screaming something in English from a second-floor window of the house across the street. With great difficulty, I guessed that she meant something like "Stop being cruel to the dogs immediately! Otherwise I'll call the police!"

I remember I was so frightened that I barely managed to answer in faltering English that the puppies must have been left there by someone, and that I was just trying to give them some food. Even then, the woman did not soften her frightening look. She did not retreat until she had given me a long lecture on the cruelty of the Japanese.

I have heard several other examples of English women in particular making a big fuss over the "cruelty" of the Japanese to animals. For example, a man crossing a busy Tokyo intersection with a heavily-laden, horse-drawn cart started whipping the horse in order to get through as quickly as possible. An English woman who happened to be passing by in an automobile stopped, jumped on him, snatched his whip, and struck him with it.

In another incident, some members of the British Society for the Prevention of Cruelty to Animals residing in Tokyo went to various hospitals to complain about the inhumane treatment of dogs being used in medical experiments. The name of this society in itself tells us something. In Japanese it is known as the gentle-sounding *Dōbutsu Aigo Kyōkai* 'Society for the Loving Protection of Animals,' but the original English name (Society for the Prevention of Cruelty to Animals) is much more polemical and even strident. Since it was founded in 1824, the members have been constantly on the lookout for possible violators.

Every year, England, the world's greatest canine paradise, exports a tremendous number of dogs to Japan, which is enjoying a "pet boom" at present. However, when Japanese cannot handle their dogs for some reason or do not want them any longer, they readily abandon them. That is why there are words in Japanese such as *sute-inu* 'abandoned dog,' *nora-inu* 'stray dog,' and *yaken-gari* 'roundup of owner-less dogs' which are not easily translatable into English. It is this practice of abandoning dogs that angers many English, people including the above-mentioned wife of the naval attaché. When this practice was reported in a popular British newspaper in 1972, it gave rise to a public outcry against exporting "poor" dogs to Japan. The issue was even taken up by the British Parliament at that time.

What, however, do the English do when they find themselves unable to care for their dogs? They either poison or shoot them.[1] They consider this the most rational and the best way for animals because it is the least painful. We Japanese, on the other hand, could not stand to shoot cute puppies. Poisoning also seems inhumane. Though we normally would not take care of or pay attention to stray dogs, we suddenly feel sorry for them when we see a dog catcher and may even try to help them get away by standing in his way. And this in spite of the fact that we all know from experience that, in overcrowded societies such as Japan, letting stray dogs run free or abandoning unwanted dogs causes many inconveniences. There is, in fact, nothing particularly praiseworthy about abandoning dogs and the English way of dealing with the problem is probably more suited to modern urban life.

Japanese Dogs and Occidental Dogs

However, what I want to consider here is not the merits and demerits of specific methods. In other words, I am not concerned with the question of how we can best keep dogs in today's society. Rather I am interested in the difference between the English mentality which holds that one should dispose of unwanted dogs with one's own hands and the Japanese psychology of abandoning dogs somewhere out of sight.

Even though we know that abandoned dogs and cats will most likely die, we still cannot bring ourselves to kill them. Hoping against hope that they might be lucky enough to be picked up by someone, we abandon these animals. Through this Japanese behavior, I hope to analyze the deep-rooted Japanese view of animals, and the fundamental Japanese attitude toward living things. By considering the contrast between abandoning and mercy killing, I shall examine how the word *cruelty* can mean different things to different nations with different cultures—in this case, the British and the Japanese.

But, in fact, the ultimate objective of this chapter is not a comparative cultural examination of the concept of cruelty. What I hope to show from this comparison is the common mistake we Japanese make of using Occidental value norms, which are primarily alien to us, as though they were universal measures. The dog example will help demonstrate this point.

Japan's modernization, or Westernization, which was a tremendous cultural transformation, did not take place through the conventional process of conquests or migrations, which involve mass movements of people; instead it took the very unusual form of the movement of "objects and books," with less of the normal direct human contact. This makes it essential for Japanese linguists to consider the problem of foreign cultures adopted mainly via language.

Let me now go back to my example: dogs. English people's love of dogs is almost fanatic. The May 8, 1971, issue of the *Asahi* newspaper published a report from London with the headline: "Series of Accidents Caused by Dogs Upsets England, Animals' Paradise." One incident reported concerned a four-year-old boy in London. One day, while completely absorbed in a game, he climbed over a fence into a neighbor's yard, where two Alsatian dogs attacked him and crushed his skull between their jaws, critically wounding him. The dogs were shot to death by the police who rushed to the scene. After the incident, the young victim's family

94

began receiving threatening letters instead of get-well wishes. One of these letters, obviously from an "animal lover" who was indignant over the shooting of the dogs by the police, contained a picture of a tombstone as well as the message "Your child will probably die soon, and that serves him right. You parents are the ones responsible for his death." About fifteen other crank letters were delivered to the parents. The boy's mother was so upset that she even fell ill. The article went on to explain that in England, if a dog owner knows that he has a dangerous animal, he is held responsible for an accident caused by the dog through his neglect, but the penalty for such an offense has never exceeded one pound. If a dog that is considered safe suddenly bites someone, the owner is not held responsible. However, the *Asahi* report concluded, since there has recently been a series of accidents caused by dogs, the Parliament itself has had to reconsider these laws.

The reason there are laws in England which seem so dog-centered to us Japanese is that canines in England are generally very well trained and in the past such accidents have been rare. This is true not just of England but applies more or less to all European countries.

In recent years, Japanese tourists have begun to travel to Europe in increasing numbers. People interested in dogs always say, after returning to Japan, how surprised they were to find dogs in Europe so docile. In Letters-to-the-Editor columns in newspapers, too, there are often letters to the effect that people in Europe are well aware of their social responsibility as citizens and train their dogs in such a way as to avoid making a public nuisance of them. For example the following letter entitled "Canine Training in Holland" appeared in the morning edition of the *Asahi* dated May 18, 1971.

> Living in Amsterdam, I often encounter scenes which would never occur in Japan, such as dogs riding streetcars. Dogs here are very well treated. But actually dogs themselves are extremely gentle and well behaved. They rarely sniff at people. I have observed such an incident only once. That was when I saw a dog on a streetcar sniff timidly at an old lady's toes. Barking is out of the question. That is why they are allowed to ride streetcars. First I thought that they might even be of different stock, but their behavior actually mirrors that of their owners. Needless to say, sniffing at people is very bad manners. It therefore follows that the owner of a dog that does such a thing is also very rude and is not qualified to keep a dog.

The writer of the above letter must really hate to be sniffed at by dogs. But joking aside, he was evidently struck by the contrast between such civilized dogs and the rude and poor-mannered ones in his homeland. Moreover, he seems to attribute the good manners of European dogs to the owners' qualifications as human beings. This is precisely the point I want to discuss below. People like the person who wrote the above letter usually argue "The fact that dogs are well trained in Europe is closely related to the high moral character of the Europeans, their sense of ethics, and their humanistic tradition." I hope to demonstrate some of the fallacies of that kind of reasoning in what follows.

Emulate Western Europe

Most Japanese visitors to the countries of Western Europe which served as models for Japan's modernization are once again deeply impressed by Europe when they find there anything different from what they have in Japan. "Lawns are immaculate; every place looks like a park. The Parisians, for example, who built a tremendous sewer system hundreds of years ago, seem to have had foresight and a sense of planning. In contrast, we Japanese . . ." goes the argument. This type of thinking seems to have infiltrated the very marrow of the Japanese today. Even scholars, who supposedly try to remain objective, cannot be said to be free of this tendency.

Lawns in Europe are indeed beautiful, but that is because the productivity of soil is so low that, if one may exaggerate, the only "weed" that grows well is grass. This fact is of course completely unknown to Japanese visitors. Japan, on the other hand, has a sub-tropical climate most of the year. The productivity of soil is so high that if we leave our lawns untouched, they will turn into weed jungles. That is why the maintenance of lawns in Japan requires a fantastic amount of labor. Compare this with Europe, where even forests have so little underbrush that one can literally ride a horse through them.

Even the great effort and expense spent on the sewer system of Paris was not necessarily due to foresight. The medieval city was ravaged by plagues and a sanitation system was built to avoid a repetition of such tragedy.

There are other examples of these misinformed comparisons. At the time of the Tokyo Olympic Games in 1964, some

Japanese made a great fuss saying that they wanted to see discontinued the display of laundry on the balconies of apartment houses, or at least of those along the New Trunk Line (Translator's note: the then new railroad line where the so-called "bullet train" runs) between Tokyo and Osaka. They were concerned that this sight, non-existent in Western Europe, might look ugly to foreign visitors.

However, the reason the wash is not hung out in Northern Europe is that the sunshine is too weak to dry much of anything. Thus in Northern Europe, the cultural pattern of hanging out the wash has never developed. Furthermore, winter is the most humid season in that part of the world and wash hung outdoors would simply freeze, while indoors it dries quickly due to the good heating systems. On the other hand, it is not at all uncommon in Southern Europe to see the wash hung out on clotheslines between houses. In fact, one often has to duck under damp laundry when out for a walk in the sunnier European countries.

In Japan too, we have strong sunshine and unlike Northern Europe, summer is the time for high humidity. It is natural and necessary for us to air our bedding and dry our laundry on the balcony. The above-cited argument for prohibiting the display of laundry disregards these facts.

Similarly, Japanese nature lovers are envious of the protection European countries give to wild animals and plants. But even this is not a product of the high social morality of the Europeans. In fact, exactly the opposite is the case. In early modern times, there was a great deal of destruction of nature in Europe. Wild animals were hunted or displaced and one species after another became extinct. The situation reached such a dangerous point that people finally had to

98

learn from this bitter experience. It is for that reason alone that they have advanced to where they are today.

In Japan, people have been blessed by the extreme abundance of nature and belated industrialization, so environmental destruction did not become an issue until just recently, two hundred years behind Europe. It will make sense if the Japanese recognize the problem which faces them today, saying, "Let's not repeat the Europeans' folly. Let's not follow in their footsteps." But saying "Let's emulate the Europeans" is wide of the mark.

But this is somewhat of a digression. Let us now return to the subject of dogs.

Different Views of Animals in Japan and England

The English are certainly good at training dogs. I have already explained that across from my house there is an official residence for the naval attaché to the British Embassy. The new family that moves in every three years never fails to bring a dog. The number of families must have reached seven or eight by now, but every single dog so far has been admirably well behaved. They do not bark or make unnecessary noise in the house and they are extremely docile when they go out for walks with their masters. They do not bark when they pass other dogs; nor do they run up to them. They just walk quietly with their masters, looking straight ahead. Needless to say, they need no leashes.[2]

In contrast we might well be embarrassed by the horrible manners of most Japanese dogs. They always jump on or bark at one another. If they are big, their masters have a hard time restraining them. Some masters are pulled so hard by their dogs that they are forced to walk quickly. Two Japanese dog owners meeting in a narrow alley are a sight to behold. If one of them happens to have a tiny, timid-looking dog, he might even turn into a side street or turn completely around. A woman owning a small dog might pick it up to protect it and walk hurriedly past.

In the hands of English people, dogs, whether German shepherds, bassets, dachshunds, terriers, or setters, learn to follow their masters quietly, as though they were all some unusual species. Fantastic is the only word for it. (Incidentally, the Americans are probably similar to the Japanese as far as the training of dogs is concerned. All the dogs owned by American families in my neighborhood are so utterly out of control that I have a hard time walking past their homes with my dog. Their German shepherds are particularly notorious).

The Japanese are good at spoiling dogs. Dogs do not respect us at all. Even dogs that were trained carefully in England get out of control after they have come to Japan and spent two or three years under Japanese ownership. What in the world causes this conspicuous difference? In my opinion, it is due to the great difference in the way the English and the Japanese view relations between humans and animals. The Japanese do not regard domestic animals such as dogs, cats, and horses as something that is totally under man's rule or subservient to man. Of course, outwardly, in daily relations to domestic animals, i.e., such activities as taking care of them, feeding them, and slaughtering them for man's use, there is no significant difference between the Japanese and English. But they are utterly different when it comes to their underlying views of what position domestic animals occupy with relation to man.

To the Japanese, the dog is a free and autonomous being. Man and dog, though fundamentally independent of each other, simply happen to cross paths. Until recently there was no custom in Japan of keeping dogs leashed or fenced in. Dogs used to walk around freely, looking for garbage or discarded food. Quite often, a dog gradually came to belong to some specific family after regularly appearing at their kitchen door to be fed. Sometimes it even happened that two or more families regarded the same dog as their own.

In Japan, a dog often has its litter under the veranda of the owner's house unbeknownst to the family. That freedom is also given to the dog. But the family does not wish to be bothered with unwanted puppies, which are thus abandoned in a place with heavy pedestrian traffic, such as at the foot of a bridge.

When a Japanese abandons unwanted puppies, his sole purpose is to put them as far away as possible from the sphere of his daily life in order to sever unnecessary ties. He does not feel he must kill them. If many people walk past, the puppies might be picked up by someone who wants them. Many Japanese dog owners have, in fact, started out unwillingly after being forced to keep abandoned puppies brought home by their children.

The English, on the other hand, consider domestic animals something that should be completely under man's rule, something that has no autonomy. Since domestic animals are subservient beings used by man, man for his part has the responsibility to take care of them from beginning to end.

The English practice of killing with their owns hands dogs that are unwanted or terminally ill is based on their belief that the life and death of such animals should be completely controlled by man, the master.

That is why when we Japanese abandon dogs, the English criticize us, saying that we are not fulfilling our responsibility as human beings. It follows from their way of thinking that mercy killing is the proper way of handling unwanted dogs. In a word, their view which, as I indicated above, *appears* very dog-centered is, in fact, totally man-centered.

What is cruel or not cruel is for man to decide, and what is more, the European concept of cruelty does not cover anything but warm-blooded beasts. The same English women who express sympathy for the dogs abandoned in Japan remark calmly that the best way to cook lobsters is to throw them alive into boiling water. Neither is it considered cruel to catch fish merely for the fun of it with no intention of using them for food. Exerting oneself for hours on the ocean in a struggle with a huge marlin is nothing but a tremendous sport. It does not even occur to them how much the fish might be suffering.

Of course, whether they are English or Japanese, people in general are not clearly conscious of the above-mentioned views of animals or life. If asked about their practices, they will perhaps rationalize them in one way or another, but such value systems, which affect people's subconsciousness, are generally well hidden under the surface.

A number of years ago, an icebound Japanese observation crew in Antarctica finally managed to escape from their base by helicopter but were forced to leave behind the huskies that they had brought from Japan. Some readers may remember the clamor that was raised at the time, both in Japan and abroad. (I think the criticism that such a measure might be hazardous to the ecology of Antarctica has some merit, but that is not the point I am considering here.) The members of the crew just could not stand the thought of killing the dogs they loved. None of them thought the dogs would live until the next year, yet they could not bring themselves to kill the animals. But lo and behold, when they returned to Showa Base one year later, two of the dogs were still alive. The men must have been very glad that they had not killed the dogs. In this case, it was not the man-oriented, man-centered way of disposing of domestic animals, but the Japanese way of handling them that won, at least from the standpoint of the dogs' happiness.[3]

Earlier I mentioned how poor the Japanese are at training dogs and making them obey orders in comparison with the English. But to view the situation from another angle, the Japanese actually have no desire to rule dogs completely. They do not think they should make them totally subservient, so they simply do not try to rule them. Furthermore, there seems to be a feeling among Japanese that since the dog is an independent creature it is all but impossible to make it obey anyway. It would of course be convenient for the Japanese, too, to have dogs who obey their masters. But we Japanese feel that although we may wish or hope to have such a dog, it is neither the duty nor the responsibility of man to train a dog to be obedient. The man-centered idea that a dog's happiness lies in being trained to obey—an idea which I am sure dogs themselves would not appreciate at all—has traditionally been foreign to the Japanese.

Naturally a view of animals peculiar to a certain culture

103

and a certain nation is not stationary or definite; neither are its origins simple and self-evident. One of the reasons the English know how to train dogs almost perfectly might be that they have done a good deal of dairy farming for a long time and thus are used to handling domestic animals. Another reason could be that since the climate necessitated the cohabitation of pets and people under the same roof in closed living quarters, dogs had to be strictly trained to preserve domestic peace.

By contrast, the Japanese civilization was never significantly dependent on domestic animals. Furthermore, Japanese living quarters have always been open due to the warm, humid climate, and it was neither necessary nor wise to live with dogs. Consequently, the patterns of coexistence which would have emerged if man and dogs had lived together in a confined space never developed in Japan.

Religion must have played a role here, also. As is well known, Christianity does not recognize animal souls, whereas traditional Japanese religions have strong elements of animism and shamanism. Japanese Buddhism, which was later added to these, even believes in metempsychosis, or transmigration of souls.

This difference between the Western Weltanschauung and ours is, in a word, a contrast between the idea of discontinuity and that of continuity. The former standpoint makes man's superiority absolute, whereas the latter makes it only relative. To the English, cruelty probably means not to treat a particular animal according to the role they have assigned to it from a man-centered viewpoint. To the Japanese, cruelty is a concept that concerns useless and unnecessary killing.

104

Importing Concepts with No Regard to the Value Systems Behind Them

I attempted the preceding argument despite the fact I am merely a linguist unfamiliar with philosophy or religion. I did so simply out of my dissatisfaction with a still prevalent tendency among Japanese people to disregard the different value systems which give meaning to individual words, to translate into Japanese certain concepts which are valid only within the framework of Western civilization, and to discuss very carelessly which is superior or inferior, the West or Japan.

I am often struck by the strange inadequacy of arguments I hear from Japanese people who are supposed to have studied Europe for a long time and in depth. It is a great misconception to think that foreign languages can be understood perfectly by means of dictionaries and grammar books. It is no exaggeration to say that the kind of knowledge which does not go beyond equating words (e.g., "*cruelty* means *zankoku* in Japanese") may cause only harm.

These overtly literal lexical and cultural equations can cause a variety of misunderstandings. Even in the realm of domestic animals the problems are not limited to dogs. Let us consider horses for a moment. Nowadays, we rarely see horses in big cities, but no doubt most Japanese are still familiar with them because of such things as equestrian competition, horses for rent at summer resorts, and horse races (which are growing more popular day by day). Middle-aged and elderly people in Japan probably remember having contact with different kinds of horses, e.g., horses for farming, work horses to draw carts, army horses, and horses that drew carriages long ago.

If an ordinary Japanese with these kinds of experiences with horses visits England, his basic concept of the types of contact between horses and people is unlikely to be changed. Of course, he might find that horseback riding is a far more important sport in England than in Japan; he might also learn many new things about derbies in the country where they originated. Nevertheless, I am sure there are very few Japanese who have ever felt that people's attitude toward horses and their view of horses are basically different in England and Japan. The reason is obviously that there are many corresponding elements: horse-drawn carts are seen in both countries, horses are still used in farming both in Japan and England, and so on.[4]

Now then, suppose a Japanese staying in London hits upon the idea of cooking horse meat for a drinking party with some friends. In Japan, horse meat is called *sakura niku* (lit., 'cherry meat') because of its red color; it is comparatively inexpensive and is widely believed to have a warming effect when eaten. It is generally known to be mixed in sausages and pressed ham. Some even say that cheap beef is sometimes sold with horse meat mixed in. With this background, it is not particularly strange if a Japanese happens to wish for horse meat in London. However, if he goes to a nearby meat market and says "I would like three pounds of horse meat," what will happen? Probably the shopkeeper will answer somewhat ill-humoredly that he does not sell such a thing. How do we account for this? The answer is simply that in England, horse meat is not considered human food. There are even regulations specifically prohibiting the sale of horse meat by regular butchers.[5]

English people seem to regard horses as man's friends, on a par with dogs. To them, the idea of eating horse meat is almost as disgusting as cannibalism. Therefore, if a Japanese customer asks an English butcher for horse meat, he will not merely be considered an eccentric; the butcher might, in fact, conclude that the Japanese must be an extremely cruel race. As far as most uses of horses and their position in social life are concerned, there seems to be little difference between Japan and England, and yet in this emotional realm of the edible and nonedible the English and the Japanese attach entirely different values to horses.

I once asked some Japanese who had visited England or had lived there for a long time what the English thought about horse meat, but none of them knew anything about it. Thus I was again made to realize how difficult it is to notice "covert culture." It is true that there are many things about foreign countries which do not become clear until one gets there. However, "covert culture" does not always become apparent though one has traveled in a country or even lived there for a long time. Unless the visitor has developed an awareness of problems from the standpoint of his own culture, he cannot see many phenomena which he might find striking once they were pointed out.

Unlike concepts used in the natural sciences, most of the concepts used in the social sciences and the humanities were originally based on phenomena observed in some particular society or societies. Thus, while they are in a sense empirical, they are also relative. It is an undeniable fact that

107

concepts in the social sciences and the humanities used by Japanese scholars and intellectuals more or less have their origins in Western Europe. These concepts, therefore, derive their values from the reality of Western Europe and not from some objective value system. Nevertheless, at least as far as I can see, these concepts originating in Western Europe have, in not a few instances, come to be accepted by us Japanese as universal measures. The reason must be, as I have repeatedly emphasized on many occasions, that the nature of language is grasped only insufficiently.

Let us compare a word to an iceberg. The tip of an iceberg visible above the ocean is supposed to be about one-seventh of its total volume. The other six-sevenths is hidden under the water. The part of reality which can be conceptualized by a word may be regarded as the tip of an iceberg rising above the water. However, to people who created a certain concept themselves, the fact that this visible part is the superstructure of the part hidden under the water is, as it were, a tacit premise. This covert part may be considered a foundation that gives the concept, i.e., the overt part, its own particular value. Even if there are two icebergs A and B more or less shaped alike above the water, it does not necessarily follow, as one can easily understand, that their shapes under the water are also similar to each other.

When a concept based on the socio-cultural reality of Western Europe is identified, as a word, with an existing Japanese concept or is given a Japanese word newly created for the purpose, what is often happening is the match-up of these overt portions only. Not only do we not see the covert part of the imported concept, but we are usually unconscious of the covert part of our own concept. Consequently, when we analyze Japanese culture, using these concepts based on such mistaken equations, it is inevitable that we go far beyond or fall short of an accurate assessment of our non-Western reality.

The Measure for the Japanese Language Should Be the Japanese Language Itself

Putting abstract discussions aside, let us turn to the field of linguistics again. In this field, one can definitely say that everywhere one looks there are inadequate statements and studies based on the manipulation of concepts that do not help explain phenomena indigenous to Japan. This situation reminds me of the Greek myth about Procrustes, who forcibly stretched or amputated the legs of travelers to make them fit the length of his bed.

Whether in the writing system,[6] the phonology,[7] or the grammar of Japanese, there are problems which cannot be solved by using Western European languages as measures, as has often been done in the past. How many times have we heard complaints about the Japanese language being inconvenient and illogical. I once called this kind of Japanese mentality *ayamareru taishō e no jikodōka-genshō*, or the phenomenon of identifying with the wrong model.[8]

In my opinion, the measure for the Japanese language should be looked for in Japanese itself, just as the measure for Japan's reality should be found in Japan's reality itself. If universalization is the objective, it can be achieved only at a higher dimension where it is possible to consider and explain both Japan and Western Europe on an equal basis. I believe universalization cannot possibly be attained by simply applying Western-European norms to Japan.

As an example of studies based on the philosophy described in this chapter, I will summarize in the next chapter a research project I have conducted for the past several years on the topic of "words for self and others."

6. Words for Self and Others

In Japanese

Whenever one person engages in dialogue with another, it becomes necessary to make clear who is speaking to whom. For example, if a native speaker of English is asked what word he uses when referring to himself, he will definitely give *I* or *me* as his answer. Likewise, a French speaker would reply that *je* or *moi* is the word he would use. If one then asks what words are used to refer to the addressee, one will learn that they are *you* in English and *tu* or *vous* in French.

In most European languages, the set of words referring to the speaker and the addressee is organized in a more or less similar way; this set is comprised of a very limited number of words called personal pronouns. This linguistic fact explains the prevalence, in the grammars of European languages, of a formula classifying first- and second-person pronouns as words which refer to the speaker and to the addressee, respectively.

In the late nineteenth century, the pioneers of modern Japanese grammar copied this classification worked out by Western grammarians. Thus they grouped such Japanese words as *watakushi*, *boku*, and *ore* together and called them "first-person pronouns," and such words as *anata*, *kimi*, and *kisama* became "second-person pronouns." This was actually quite understandable in the light of the stage of linguistics at that time, but this analysis has persisted. Even today Japanese grammar books contain remarks to the effect that first- and second-person pronouns in Japanese are numerous and complex or that third-person pronouns are not well developed in Japanese. This is precisely because the traditional view of pronouns based on Western European grammatical analysis has survived to the present.

I have spoken out against this traditional view on numerous occasions over the past several years,[1] arguing that the classification of *watakushi/anata*, *boku/kimi*, etc., as personal pronouns was the result of blindly accepting analyses derived from the studies of other languages, languages which are structurally different from Japanese in many respects. Such classification is highly vulnerable to error, and I contend that it is in fact wrong, since it is incongruent with the linguistic facts in Japanese.

It is true that as a rule when a person speaks in English he calls himself "I" and his hearer "you," barring exceptional cases.[2] However, things are completely different in Japanese. For example, in Japan today, when a father talks to his children at home, he very often refers to himself as *Otōsan* 'Father' or *Papa*. He would normally say *Otōsan no iu koto o kiki-nasai* 'Listen to Father,' instead of *Boku/Watashi no iu koto o kiki-nasai* 'Listen to me.' If a nephew or a niece comes to his house, the same man then calls himself *Ojisan* 'Uncle,' as in *Kurisumasu ni Ojisan ga jitensha o purezento-shiyō* 'Uncle will give you a bicycle for Christmas.' Grandparents, talking to their grandchildren, or even to their sons or daughters-in-law, regularly call themselves *Ojīsan* 'Grandfather' and *Obāsan* 'Grandmother,' as in *Oi, chotto Ojīsan no kata o monde-kurenai ka* 'Say, won't you massage Grandfather's shoulders?'

Elementary school teachers say to their students *Sā, Sensei no hō o mite* 'Now, look at Teacher.' Doctors and nurses, when talking to young patients, sometimes even refer to themselves as *Oisha-san* 'Doctor' and *Kangofu-san* 'Nurse,' using their occupational titles. Young girls often refer to themselves by names instead of using *watashi* 'I.' A little girl named Yumi, for example, might say *Yumi wa kore kirai yo* 'Yumi doesn't like this.'

Terms used to designate the addressee are not always restricted to personal pronouns such as *anata* and *kimi* either. Indeed, investigations into actual usage make it clear that personal pronouns appear only on very limited occasions.

For example, no one would use such pronouns as *anata* 'you' when talking to senior members of the family, e.g., parents or older siblings. When Japanese talk to their teachers or to their superiors at work, they address them as *Sensei* 'Teacher,' or *Kachō(-san)* 'Section Chief,' and are unlikely to use *anata*. Despite the fact that *anata* is generally considered a more polite word (though not part of *keigo* 'honorific language') than *kimi*, *omae*, and *kisama* (all of which are different ways of saying *you*), it is really a word not easily used when addressing persons of higher status. As I will later explain in detail, it is not an exaggeration to say that present-day Japanese has no personal pronoun which can be used to refer to superiors. *Anata-sama*, another polite word meaning "you," is a word used to indicate respectful aloofness when addressing a stranger, rather than an individual whose status we know to be higher than our own. It cannot be used when speaking to someone whom we can clearly place as a superior, for example, a teacher or senior member of a group. If no suitable pronoun exists which we may use to address such people, what expressions other than pronouns do we actually use when we must directly refer to our listeners?

As in the case of speaker designation, words representing family relationships may be used for the addressee, too. Beginning with *Otōsan* 'Father' and *Okāsan* 'Mother,' other kinship terms such as *Ojīsan* 'Grandfather,' *Obasan* 'Aunt,' and *Nīsan* 'Older Brother' are frequently used instead of pronouns. These terms have many variations, familiar forms, and diminutives. Futhermore, their use is often extended to persons outside the family who are actually not related to the speaker.

Occupational titles as *Sensei* 'Teacher,' *Oisha-san* 'Doctor,' and *Kangofu-san* 'Nurse' may be used with reference to the addressee as well as to the speaker. In fact, their use is even more prevalent with reference to the addressee, especially as part of the formula "such-and-such-*ya-san*."[3] Under this formula, almost all occupations may be used to refer to the addressee. If the speaker knows the addressee's occupation, he can refer to the latter as *Yaoya-san* 'Mr. Greengrocer,' *Denkiya-san* 'Mr. Electrician,' *Gomiya-san* 'Mr. Garbage Collector,' *Uekiya-san* 'Mr. Gardener,' and *Sakan'ya-san* 'Mr. Plasterer' without ever using a personal pronoun. In businesses which deal with customers, the word *Okyaku-sama*, or *Okyaku-san*, 'Mr. Customer' is widely used.

In short, present-day Japanese first- and second-person personal pronouns, considered more numerous than those of European languages, are actually not used very much. Not only that, there is a definite tendency to avoid their use as often as possible and to carry on conversations using some other words to designate speaker and addressee. Since European languages each have only one or two first-person and second-person pronouns, and since these are repeatedly used every time a conversation takes place, they are obviously quite different in nature from pronouns in Japanese.

Suppose we faithfully apply to Japanese the concept developed by Western grammarians that words which point to the speaker and the addressee are first- and second-person pronouns, respectively. Oddly enough, we will then have to say that, in Japanese, most kinship terms and innumerable occupational titles are all personal pronouns. They will in fact overshadow words such as *watashi*, *anata*, etc., hitherto called personal pronouns. This would be a very strange analysis indeed. It proves that calling *watashi*, *ore*, *omae*, and *anata* personal pronouns is a practice detached from the realities of the Japanese language and merely represents an idea translated verbatim from alien grammars.

Since the so-called Japanese personal pronouns in the narrow sense do not form an independent word group either morphologically or functionally, there is no reason for treating them separately. Rather, they should be classified, together with kinship terms, position terms, etc., into the categories of all words used by the speaker with reference to himself and to the addressee. These categories will not be dominated by pronominal forms and may be more adequately called *jishōshi* 'terms of self-reference' and *taishōshi* 'address terms,' respectively. Words referring to others who appear in dialogues should be called *tashōshi* 'terms of reference.'[4]

It will be necessary to study *jishōshi* and *taishōshi* (and *ta-*

shōshi) on the basis of observable data. What kinds of words are used under what circumstances when a speaker refers to himself or to his listener in a specific language community? We must discover the sociolinguistic rules that govern the selection of a particular form. In the following sections, I will focus on Japanese as it is spoken today. But prior to this, in order to establish the point of departure for my analysis, I will very briefly explain the nature and the historical background of personal pronouns in European languages.

In Indo-European Languages

Languages which I have so far referred to by imprecise terms such as European languages and Western European languages linguistically constitute a group called the Indo-European languages. Long ago there presumably existed one relatively uniform Proto-Indo-European language, which has subsequently, at different stages of history, branched off into many different languages. At present, this group consists of not only such languages as English, German, and French, with which we Japanese are most familiar, but also the languages of northern Europe (with the exception of Finland) and the Slavic countries. It covers an enormous area, extending as far as Greece, Iran, and part of India.

Since these languages started out as one, even today they share many similar words and expressions. For example, even amateurs can easily detect the similarity in words from these languages that are still so much alike in form. Let us look at the words for "mother": *mother* in English, *Mutter* in German, *mère* in French, *madre* in Spanish, *mat'* in Russian.

Even when words do not immediately reveal any mutual

correspondence, if we go back in history and examine old books and other data, we often discover that they were once very similar in form and in fact shared the same origin. For example, in English, one of the Germanic languages, "male parent" is *father*, which corresponds to *Vater* in German. Since each of these two words begins with the sound [f], this formal similarity makes it comparatively easy for us to see that they must be derived from a single earlier form. However, if one looks at other branches of the Indo-European language family, the Romance languages, for example, we find that *father* is *père* in French and *padre* in Spanish. Most people can probably accept the idea fairly readily that these two words, both beginning with [p], share the same origin, but they might feel suspicious if they hear that the words are intimately related to the two Germanic words *father* and *Vater*.

Nevertheless, comparative linguists, with their scientific techniques, have made a detailed comparative study of the existing old materials written in languages belonging to these two language groups, and have been able to demonstrate that in the Germanic languages the word-initial [p] uniformly changed to [f] a very long time ago. It has also become clear that the French and Spanish words meaning "father" both derive from Latin *pater*, which was after all very close in form to the Old-German word for "father." The same techniques have also established that English *fish* and German *Fisch* on the one hand and French *poisson* and Spanish *pez* on the other correspond to each other.

I have tried to demonstrate with some very simple examples that most European languages share the same origin, and that they even now abound in instances of mutual correspondence both in form and in meaning. In fact, exactly the same statement may be made about personal pronouns.

For example, in modern English, the equivalent of the Japanese *watakushi* is *I*. In German, it is *ich*; in Dutch, it is *ik*. Although it may seem at first that these personal pronouns do not share much in common, actually they do. English *I* used to be written *i* in the early Modern Ages and pronounced [i:] instead of [ai]. Farther back in time, in the Middle Ages, the word had a consonant at the end and was pronounced [itʃ] or [iʃ]. In Old English, the most archaic form of English of which written records exist, the word was spelled *ic* and was presumably pronounced [ik].

This leaves no room for doubt that English *I* derives from the same original form as the first-person pronouns in German and Dutch. It is now believed that first-person pronouns in these so-called Germanic languages can all be traced to a Proto-Germanic form, which must have been something like *ik*.

On the other hand, if we turn to the Romance languages, *I* is *je* in French, *yo* in Spanish, and *io* in Portuguese in their modern forms. It has been determined that all of these are corrupt forms of Latin *ego*. This Latin form and Greek *egō* converge with the above-cited hypothetical Proto-Germanic word *ik*. When data on other Indo-European language groups are also considered, it becomes clear that the word meaning "I" in Proto-Indo-European must have been something more or less like *ego*.

Now, what I originally set out to say about first-person pronouns in Indo-European languages was that, although today each of these languages seems to be using a different word meaning "I", all these words can be traced to one and the same origin. I also wish to point out that this seemingly simple fact is really quite remarkable. It means that in the Indo-European language family the same word has been used as a first-person pronoun continuously and consistently for thousands of years. Just as a person retains his identity despite physical changes as he grows from babyhood through childhood to adulthood, the so-called identity of the first-person pronoun in Indo-European languages has not changed since the beginning of history. This point, which I believe has not received much attention in the past, really presents a striking contrast to the Japanese situation which will be discussed in detail later.

In comparison with first-person pronouns, the history of second-person pronouns in Indo-European languages is a little more complex, but leaving minor details aside, the oldest form seems to have been something like *tu*. And this form remains in present-day Romance languages almost unchanged. Consider, for example, *tu* in French and *tu* in Italian. Moreover, Russian has *tui*. German *du* only shows a change in the voiced quality of the initial sound. Even in English, this same old pronoun has survived until recently in the form of the familiar *thou*.

It is true that second-person pronouns in Indo-European languages as they are spoken today are a little complicated because of the influx of pronouns unrelated to the *tu* forms. Nevertheless, if one limits discussion to the *tu*-derivatives, one can say, as in the case of first-person pronouns, that the same word has retained its identity continuously for thousands of years.

Japanese Personal Pronouns

When compared with first- and second-person pronouns in European languages, which have histories of thousands of years, the short lives of Japanese personal pronouns stand out in sharp contrast. So-called first-person pronouns in standard modern Japanese, such as *watakushi* and *boku*, do not date back to Old Japanese. In fact, *boku* is a newcomer whose history in spoken Japanese is only slightly over one hundred years long. The use of *kimi*, *omae*, *anata*, *kisama*, and other terms as personal pronouns which refer to the addressee does not date back to Old Japanese either, although some of these terms may have been present earlier as members of noun categories.

In Japanese, since the beginning of history, new personal pronouns for the speaker, as well as for the hearer, have been created one after another in rapid succession. Each new term has replaced an earlier one. Furthermore, every new pronoun has been borrowed from another category where it had a concrete meaning. *Watakushi* and *boku*, which refer to the speaker in standard modern Japanese, and *kimi* and *kisama*, which refer to the addressee, are all good examples of this. The original meanings of these words are *watakushi* 'private or personal,' *boku* 'servant,' *kimi* 'lord,' and *kisama* 'noble person.' Other personal pronouns such as *anata* 'you < that direction,' *omae* 'you < front,' *kochira* 'I < this direction,' and *donata* 'who < what direction' were originally demonstratives referring to places or directions. These demonstratives were then diverted to a suggestive and euphemistic use to indicate indirectly persons in those places or directions. Japanese pronouns are thus markedly different from their Indo-

120

European counterparts, such as *ego/tu* in Latin or *I/you* in English, which have been used from the beginning exclusively to signal the speaker or the addressee no matter how far back we may go in history.

The person who was the first to discuss the historical changes of Japanese personal pronouns in detail was Kanae Sakuma.[5] His study not only highlighted the rapid changes in the pronominal system, but also pointed to a remarkable fact concerning the pattern of vicissitudes of personal pronouns. That is, whenever a new pronoun for speaker self-reference comes into use, it first connotes the sense of humility the speaker feels toward the addressee, but as its usage continues, it gradually begins to express the speaker's sense of superiority to the addressee, and finally becomes a word which can be used only when the speaker looks down on the addressee, thus falling out of general use.

For example, *boku* 'I' was a literary word primarily used in the Tokugawa Period (1603–1868) in *kambun*, i.e., Japanese written in the classical Chinese style. At that time it meant 'your servant' and was used to convey one's inferiority to the addressee. Its use in spoken Japanese came later, during the Meiji era (1868–1912). Now, over a hundred years after the beginning of the Meiji period, *boku* is considered inappropriate for use when speaking to superiors or on formal occasions.

In May, 1952, the National Language Council in Japan submitted to the Minister of Education a proposal entitled "Kore kara no keigo" [Honorific language for the future]. Paragraph three of the section entitled "Words for Self-Reference" states that *boku* 'I' is used by male students, and that even they should be encouraged to replace it with *watashi* 'I' once they go out into the world. Paragraph three

121

of the section entitled "Words of Address" explains that the use of *kimi* 'you' and *boku* 'I' should be limited to very close relationships, and that in most cases it would be desirable to use the more standard forms *watakushi* 'I' and *anata* 'you.' The proposal obviously indicates that *boku* is regarded as an expression which is less than respectful to the addressee.

Strictly speaking, however, this document was not based on an accurate observation of the linguistic facts of Japanese; it contains elements which suggest that the council made a deliberate but premature attempt to democratize the Japanese language, probably encouraged by the Allied occupation forces. The document should therefore be taken with a grain of salt. For example, when Eisaku Satō was prime minister, he always used *watakushi* in answering questions at the Diet but switched to *boku* at press conferences and informal interviews; this leads us to conclude that at least to persons of greater age the difference between these two words is a real one.

Now, according to Sakuma, the directional shifts in second-person pronouns are exactly the opposite of those in first-person pronouns. For example, expressions such as *temae* 'you' and *kisama* 'you' originally showed respect to the addressee. With the passage of time, however, these terms gradually began to imply contempt, eventually becoming words to curse and abuse the addressee. At best, they are rough expressions allowed only between close friends.[6]

Earlier I mentioned the rapid vicissitudes of Japanese personal pronouns. These rises and falls are brought about not only by a gradual replacement of old pronouns by new ones, but also by corruption of word meaning as explained in the preceding pages.

122

These transformations pointed out by Sakuma with reference to Japanese personal pronouns are what I would call "taboo-type changes." In linguistics, a taboo is an act of avoiding a direct reference to a certain object or fact, out of fear or shyness or for religious reasons. When reference to these objects or facts becomes absolutely necessary, they are spoken of indirectly or suggestively by means of other words.

Japanese mountain people call a bear *oyaji* 'the old man' and Slavs refer to the same animal as *medved'* 'honey eater' without using its real name; these are good examples of taboos. Actually English *bear* and German *Bär* both share the same origin with *brown*. Because of a taboo prohibiting direct reference to bears as such, a word which meant something like "the brown one" was used to make indirect reference to the animal.

When taboo-based indirect expressions, whose primary characteristic is euphemistic suggestiveness, are used for a long time, they gradually lose this quality. They are therefore destined to be replaced one after the other by newer words. The fact that so-called personal pronouns in present-day Japanese are not really words which directly indicate either the speaker or the addressee, but words that indirectly refer to them, as well as the fact that in the history of the language they have frequently replaced one another, definitely shows that they are taboo-related. Indeed, the Japanese have a tendency even today to do without personal pronouns in conversation whenever possible.

In contrast, when one considers that the same personal pronouns have been continuously used in Indo-European languages for thousands of years and that the grammars of these languages require their use in virtually every conversation, one naturally begins to suspect the validity of classifying Japanese "personal pronouns" in the same linguistic category.

Japanese Terms of Self-Reference and Address

Now we finally come to the point where we are to examine the rules that exist in Japanese today, especially in the Tokyo dialect, with respect to the use of terms for self-reference and address. But prior to this, I wish to establish once again what *terms of self-reference* and *address terms* mean. Terms of self-reference include all the words with which the speaker refers to himself. In Japanese, the first-person pronouns constitute only a small portion of this category. Address terms include all the words the speaker uses with reference to the addressee, and have two uses which are somewhat different in nature.

One is the vocative, which is used when the speaker wishes to attract the addressee's attention or appeal to him emotionally. In Indo-European languages, the vocative used to be treated independently as one of the inflectional cases of nouns. For example, in Latin, the noun *dominus* 'master' had a vocative form *domine* 'O Master!' Likewise in Greek, the vocative of *kyrios* 'master' was *kyrie* 'O Master!' In present-day European languages, the vocative has all but disappeared as a formally distinct case. In Japanese, the vocative form of a noun may often be indicated by such expressions as *Chichi yo* "O Father!" but this cannot possibly be called a modern colloquial usage. The vocative includes the use of animal names to express affection or anger toward the addressee. In Turkey, as well as in Europe, loved ones are sometimes addressed as "lark," "piglet," and "chick." In Japan, we sometimes use such words as *inu* 'dog,' *buta* 'pig,' and *ōkami* 'wolf' when addressing someone we hate. A cross-cultural study of vocatives expressing love or hate would be fascinating, but here I will not pursue the issue any further.

Address terms also have what some Occidental anthropologists call a "pronominal use."[7] Here, a word used as the subject or object of a sentence actually indicates the addressee. The name is due to the fact that in Indo-European languages, it is usually a second-person form that serves as subject or object in a sentence referring to the addressee. For example, when an English-speaking child is angry at his mother, he says "I hate you!" A Japanese-speaking child would say *Okāsan nante kirai*, lit., 'I hate Mother.' *You* and *Okāsan* 'Mother' here are address terms in their pronominal use.

Now that the definitions have been provided, let us see what rules operate in Japanese when these terms are actually used. First, let us consider the data gathered from a forty-year-old male elementary school teacher, one of the people I interviewed for this study. Figure 9 is not an exhaustive list of the subject's terms for self-reference and address. I simply asked him what terms he used in talking to certain persons under normal circumstances and listed his answer to each question. With respect to some persons, he readily gave me more than one variant. He told me that in such a case he generally shifted the usage from one term to another, depending on the occasion.

Figure 9 shows that the subject uses seven different terms for self-reference: *watakushi* 'I,' *boku* 'I,' *ore* 'I,' *Ojisan* 'Uncle,'

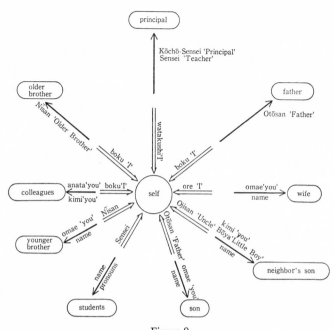

Figure 9

Otōsan 'Father,' *Sensei* 'Teacher,' and *Nīsan* 'Older Brother.'
As for address terms, he uses the names of the addressees,
Ojīsan 'Grandfather,' *Otōsan* 'Father,' *Nīsan* 'Older Brother,'
Sensei 'Teacher,' and *Bōya* 'Little Boy,' in addition to second-
person pronouns such as *anata*, *omae*, and *kimi*.

This man does not have as many relatives as he might. For
example, he has no living grandmother. Furthermore, if
we extend our investigation to incorporate the other interpersonal relationships which he has, we will discover even
more address terms. Figure 9 obviously does not include all
the terms for self or address terms that this person uses.
Nevertheless, it probably lists most of the important ones.

126

After examining people of different ages, social positions, and occupations in my attempt to discover a pattern, I have come to find rather orderly rules governing the terms of self-reference and address used by Japanese today.[8] At the base is the concept of opposition between superiors (or persons of higher status) and inferiors (or persons of lower status). This is probably only to be expected in view of the system of honorific language in Japanese, but the uses of terms for self-reference and address in Japanese interpersonal relations also reflect this idea of polarity well.

I next discovered that any Japanese dialogue, even when it takes place in a nonfamily context, can ultimately be regarded as a variation of the basic family dialogue pattern.

Between Relatives

I will begin by analyzing the structures of terms for self-reference and address used among kin. Figure 10 shows the status relationships within the Japanese family. In Japanese society, people belonging to an older generation are all considered to have higher status than the members of a younger generation; among people of the same generation, relative age determines relative status. The only exception is in the case of married couples. Between husband and wife, a difference in age is of little importance; relative status appears to be determined by other factors. Here I will tentatively treat spouses as equals.

(1) The speaker cannot use a personal pronoun to address or directly refer to a relative above the dividing line. For example, it would be strange to call one's father *anata* 'you.' It is also impossible to ask him such a question as

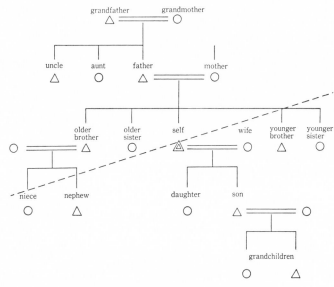

Figure 10

In dialogues with family members above the
dividing line, one can use only kinship terms
as address terms, whereas one cannot use
kinship terms to refer to oneself. In dialogues
with family members below the dividing line,
one cannot use kinship terms as address terms,
but can use kinship terms to refer to oneself.

Kono hon anata no 'Is this book yours?' Exactly the same
thing can be said about speech to one's older brother, aunt,
etc. One can, however, use a personal pronoun to address or
refer to any relative below the line of division.

(2) The speaker normally calls people above the line by
a kinship term. For example, one addresses one's mother as
Okāsan 'Mother' and says to one's grandfather *Ojisan no hige*

wa nagai ne, lit., 'How long Grandfather's beard is!'

One does not use kinship terms when speaking to persons below the line. For example, one cannot say **Oi, Otōto*, lit., 'Hey, Younger Brother!' to one's younger brother, nor can one ask one's daughter **Musume wa doko ni iku no*, lit., 'Where is Daughter going?'

(3) The speaker cannot address a person above the line by name alone. On the other hand, it is permissible to address a person below the line in that way. English differs from Japanese in that one can address one's older siblings by their names alone.

(4) The speaker can call himself by his own name when talking to a person above the line, but does not normally do so in a dialogue with a person below the line. For example, a daughter called Yoshiko may say to her mother, *Yoshiko kore kirai yo*, lit., 'Yoshiko does not like this,' meaning 'I don't like this,' but a mother never speaks like that to her daughter. In the following passage from Doppo Kunikida's short story "Shōnen no hiai" [The sorrow of a youth], although it is not, strictly speaking, a dialogue between members of a family, a male servant is referring to himself by his name while talking to his master's nephew:

> I believe I was about eleven then. One day a servant called Tokujirō told me he was going somewhere amusing that night. He would be glad to take me along if I was interested.
>
> "Where are we going?" I asked.
>
> "Don't even ask. It doesn't matter where, does it? If Toku offers to take you someplace, it's got to be a good place," answered Tokujirō with a smile.

In this story, the eleven-year old protagonist calls Toku-jirō simply "Toku." In the passage quoted, Tokujirō also refers to himself as "Toku" in speaking to his young master, but, on the other hand, speaks of himself as *washi* 'I' when talking to a young waitress with whom he is intimate, even in this boy's presence.

(5) The speaker talking to someone below the line can call himself by the kinship term which shows his relationship to the addressee as seen from the latter's perspective, but he cannot do so when talking to a person above the line. For example, in a dialogue between an older brother and a younger brother, the former can call himself *Nisan* 'Older Brother,' but the latter does not refer to himself as *Otōto-chan* 'Younger Brother.'

In Japanese, therefore, whereas words denoting 'father,' 'mother,' 'grandmother,' 'older brother,' 'older sister,' 'uncle,' and 'aunt' can serve as terms for self, words denoting 'child,' 'grandchild,' 'younger brother,' 'younger sister,' 'son,' 'daughter,' 'nephew,' and 'niece' cannot.

Of the above rules, (1), (2), and (3) are concerned with address terms, and (4) and (5) with terms of self-reference. All of the five are based on the line of division between positions of higher and lower status within the family, and these rules govern the uses of all terms for self-reference and address among kin. Of course, these are general rules which might sometimes be disregarded by the individuals of a particular family. For example, a recent trend in urban areas is for sisters close in age to call each other by their names alone.

In rule (5) above, I used the expression "words denoting 'father,' etc." The reason is that words which are actually used as terms for self-reference and address vary with each family, depending on social class, age, and family tradition. The forms *Otōsama*, *Otōsan*, *Tōsan*, *Tōchan*, and *Papa*, for example, all denote 'father,' and other kin terms also have various forms.

Interestingly enough, however, within a specific family, the address term used by a speaker when talking to someone higher in the family hierarchy is identical to the term of self-reference used by the latter. That is, if a particular child addresses his father as "Papa," the latter calls himself "Papa," too, and not *"Otōsan,"* when talking to the child. From this, one can formulate the following general rule: within a given family group, a higher status member refers to himself with the same term which an inferior uses to address him.

Outside the Family

The same rules that govern the uses of terms for self-reference and address in dialogues within the family unit apply almost unchanged to social situations outside the family.

(1) For example, under normal circumstances, one cannot call one's teacher or boss by personal pronouns such as *anata* 'you.' One may say to one's teacher *Sensei no okusama okagen ikaga desu ka*, lit., 'How is Teacher's wife?' to mean 'How is your wife?' But it is improper to ask *Anata no okusama . . .* , lit., 'How is your wife?' On the other hand, it is perfectly all right for a boss to ask a subordinate *Kimi no okusan yoku natta ka ne* 'Is your wife feeling better?'

(2) It is normal to address someone of higher social posi-

tion by the name of that position, such as *Sensei* 'Teacher' or *Kachō* 'Section Chief.' But the reverse is not true. For example, a teacher cannot address a student **Oi, Seito*! 'Hey, Student!' This reflects the same rule governing the family situation explained earlier where an older brother cannot address a younger brother **Oi, Otōto*! 'Hey, Younger Brother!'[9] The same criteria apply to the use of other pairs of opposites such as *senpai-kōhai*.† A *kōhai*, for example, may ask a *senpai, Senpai, hitotsu ikaga desu ka* 'Shall I pour you a drink, Senpai?' but not vice versa.

(3) The line of division is carefully observed with reference to the use of surnames. It would be highly unusual to call one's teacher or boss by his surname without including his occupational title. One must normally say *Tanaka-sensei*, lit., 'Teacher Tanaka,' *Yamada-kachō*, lit., 'Section Chief Yamada,' etc. These days, some so-called democratic firms and open-minded teachers seem to allow the use of surnames with only *-san*, lit., 'Mr., Miss, Mrs.,' attached.

(4) When speaking to a superior, the speaker may refer to himself by his surname alone, as in *Kachō, kore wa zehi Yamamoto ni omakase kudasai*, lit., 'Section Chief, by all means let [me] Yamamoto handle this,' but the reverse never occurs. The use of one's own surname to refer to oneself usually takes place in more or less dramatic situations where one volunteers to handle a challenging job.

(5) As for calling oneself by the word representing one's own social position or capacity, a teacher talking to his students can refer to himself as *Sensei* 'Teacher,' but students

†A *senpai* is 'an earlier graduate of the same school,' and a *kōhai* 'a later graduate of the same school.' They are typically Japanese terms in that they reflect the Japanese view of society, which determines each person's place in relation to others in terms of social position, age, seniority, etc.

132

SANTARŌ FUJI

By Sanpei Satō

1. "I have a *kōhai* in that firm. I think I'll stop by to see how he is."

2. "Hi!"
   "Nice to see you! Please sit down!"

3. "How have you been, *Senpai*?"

4. "How have *you* been?"

From the evening edition of *The Asahi*, January 23, 1973.

Figure 11

talking to a teacher cannot call themselves *Seito 'Students.' As mentioned earlier, doctors, nurses, policemen, and others may call themselves *Oisha-san* 'Doctor,' *Kangofu-san* 'Nurse,' *Omawari-san* 'Policeman,' etc., when speaking to children.[10] *Senpai* 'an earlier graduate of the same school,' too, may be used as a term for self, as in *Senpai ga kore hodo itte mo wakaran no ka*, lit., 'Don't you understand your *senpai* after all this explanation?' Even *Okyaku-san* 'Guest' may be used as a term of self-reference, as seen in the passage from *Kakka* [His excellency], a play by Hideji Hōjō, which is quoted below.

In this play, there is a scene where the famous chairman of the Nittaku Company is reported to be coming to an inn in a remote mountainous region. Not only the innkeeper but dignitaries such as the village mayor, the stationmaster, and the local member of the House of Representatives are excitedly making preparations to welcome him in the grandest manner possible. The aged chairman, however, arrives at the inn via the mountain pass behind the village in a rickety carriage that looks like it is ready to be retired from service. As a shabby-looking traveler, he is relegated to a dirty room in the old wing of the inn. Later the mistake is discovered, and His Excellency is hurriedly shown to a large room where a banquet in his honor is about to begin. The old man, who hates geisha parties, however, returns unnoticed to the same dirty room in the old wing. Oyuki, a maid at the inn, begins the following dialogue with an exclamation of surprise.

> Oyuki: Goodness, you've been given another room in the new building, you know.
>
> His Excellency: I have? Don't they remember that *Okyaku-san* ['Gentleman Guest'] insisted he preferred this room? . . . [hearing the distant sounds of the banquet] Is that the room I was in?
>
> Oyuki: How come you are back already, sir?
>
> His Excellency: *Okyaku-san* feels much more comfortable here.

In this play, the old man called "His Excellency" refers to himself as *Okyaku-san* only when he talks to the young girl Oyuki. When he speaks to others, he refers to himself as *washi* 'I.'

Fictive Use of Kinship Terms

Calling a nonrelative by a kinship term is known in anthropology as the fictive use of such terms. This practice is found in every language, though its extent may vary from one language to another. English, as we will see later, is no exception.

In Japanese, precisely because the use of personal pronouns is extremely restricted, the custom of calling nonrelatives by kinship terms seems particularly widespread. The most common kinship terms used this way are 'grandfather,' 'grandmother,' 'uncle,' 'aunt,' 'older brother,' and 'older sister.' Words referring to father and mother are rarely used, at least in the standard Tokyo dialect.

In fictive usage, too, Japanese stands in marked contrast to European languages. The difference is that in Japanese, a kinship term may be used in nonkin relationships to refer to oneself as well as to refer to the addressee. That is, Japanese is rich in the fictive use of kinship terms as terms of self-reference.

The following is the general principle upon which the fictive use of kinship terms is based: the speaker considers himself as the starting point to establish, on the basis of age and sex, what the hearer would be to him if they were related and to choose appropriate kinship terms for the hearer and for himself accordingly. For example, a young person may call an unrelated old person *Ojīsan* 'Grandfather' or *Obāsan* 'Grandmother,' or address a middle-aged man as *Ojisan*

'Uncle.' When speaking to someone younger, the speaker may refer to himself or herself as *Ojisan* 'Uncle' or *Onēsan* 'Older Sister.' In all radio or TV programs for children produced by the Japan Broadcasting Corporation (NHK), the emcee always refers to himself or herself according to this formula, for instance, *Uta no Obasan*, lit., 'Singing Aunt' and *Taisō no Onīsan*, lit., 'Older Brother Who Does Calisthenics.'

Even though this is a fictive use of kinship terms, as long as the terms are used, they are subject to all the rules that apply to their regular use. Therefore kinship terms denoting such junior positions as *Musuko* 'Son,' *Segare* 'Son,' *Mago* 'Grandchild,' *Oi* 'Nephew,' and *Mei* 'Niece' may not be used by persons of higher status than the addressee. The only exception is *Musume-san* 'Daughter,' used in addressing unrelated young girls. (I have no definitive explanation to offer for this irregularity, but have proposed tentative hypotheses elsewhere.[11]) If this is the case, do Japanese ever use kinship terms fictively to address nonkin who are clearly younger than the speaker? The answer is yes, but it is done by cleverly evading the restriction limiting such address.

Let me cite a concrete example. Suppose one Sunday a little girl in a park is found lost and crying, unable to find her parents. If an adult happens to pass by, what will he or she say to the girl? It would be quite natural for the passerby to say, "Don't cry. What's *Onēchan*'s ['Big Sister's'] name? Who was *Onēchan* with?" If the child is a boy, *Onēchan* will be replaced by *Onīchan* 'Big Brother.' This same adult, referring to himself or herself, will use *Obasan* 'Aunt,' *Onīsan* 'Older Brother,' etc., depending on his or her own age and sex, as in "*Obasan* will find *Onēchan*'s papa."

This ordinary, commonplace utterance is, however, really strange. Calling oneself *Obasan* 'Aunt' can be explained as an example of the regular fictive use of kinship terms, but calling the little child *Onēchan* 'Big Sister' cannot be explained in the same way.

The fictive use of kinship terms is based on the hypothetical treatment of the addressee, a stranger, as a relative. Thus, in order for the speaker to be able to call the addressee *Onēchan* 'Big Sister,' the latter would at least have to be older than the former.

To understand the operations of this second fictive use of kinship terms, we must return to the family, for whose members kinship terms were originally intended. Let us examine once again the primary uses of terms of self-reference and address. Only then can we see that this second type of fictive usage is, after all, an extension of one particular use of kinship terms within the family.

In present-day Japanese, specifically in the Tokyo dialect, the use of terms of self-reference and address in conversation are complex beyond imagination. Nevertheless, there are consistent rules governing usage. And this is based on the patterns found within the family.

Now, if we carefully observe dialogues between family members, which happen to set patterns for dialogues between nonrelatives, we notice some uses of kinship terms which, though we ourselves take them for granted, might sound extremely odd to others. The first of these that come to mind are such practices as a mother calling her own son *Onīchan* 'Big Brother,' or a father calling his father *Ojīsan* 'Grandfather' instead of *Otōsan* 'Father.'

The proper use of kinship terms takes the speaker as the

137

starting point. Accordingly, someone who is a father from the viewpoint of his child is a husband from the viewpoint of his wife. In spite of this, in many Japanese homes, wives call their husbands *Papa* or *Otōsan* 'Father.' That is actually very odd indeed.

The uses of kinship terms as illustrated by these examples may be called their "secondary fictive use." It does not correctly reflect the family relationship between the speaker and the addressee. Thus, it has something in common with the primary fictive use of kinship terms, whereby one calls oneself *Ojisan* 'Uncle' or *Onīsan* 'Older Brother' when talking to a child to whom one is not related.

The kind of fictiveness operating when a woman calls her husband by a word denoting 'father' or her daughter by a word denoting 'older sister,' is nonetheless different in nature from the simpler type of fictiveness whereby one simulates a blood relationship with a nonrelative.

In order to comprehend this difference, it is necessary first of all to know that kinship terms constitute a special word group which might be designated as "egocentric particulars."[12]

Suppose I point to a pencil on my desk now and ask someone "What's this?" The answer will most surely be "It's a pencil." If I point to a cat curled up in the corner of the room and ask someone what that is, the answer is likely to be "It's a cat." As seen in these examples, words signifying certain objects (or phenomena) are, in most cases, the same for everyone within a specific language community. In fact, in order for a language to be socially effective as a means of communication, each object must be referred to by one and the same word (or sign).

138

However, not every word represents the same object to everyone. Some objects are referred to by different names, depending on the speaker's perspective. Let me illustrate this point with the pencil from the previous example. If I point to the pencil and ask "What's this?" the addressee will normally answer "That's a pencil." That is to say, the same object, the pencil, is referred to as *this* by me, and as *that* by the addressee. Thus, demonstratives such as *this* and *that* are the type of words which reflect changes in the relationship between the object in question and the speaker. Words such as *right* and *left* function that way, also. The direction which I call *left* is *right* for someone facing me. Each language has a number of words such as *this-that* and *right-left* which are unclear as to what they specifically indicate until one learns who is using them and what the spatial relationship is between the speaker and the object in question. The same object therefore will be referred to by different terms, depending upon speaker position. These words are called "egocentric particulars."

In contrast, other words such as *enpitsu* 'pencil' and *neko* 'cat' are sociocentric, as it were. In the society where Japanese is spoken, the word *neko* 'cat' is known to represent one specific object. *Neko* always refers to a cat no matter who uses the word or where the speaker stands in relation to the cat in question. Society's definition of the term, not an individual speaker's relation to the object being spoken of, determines its use.

On the other hand, *migi* 'right' and *hidari* 'left' are called "egocentric words"; they cannot refer to anything specific until we know whose right or whose left, i.e., until we know who the speaker is and where he is. Japanese words which belong to this category are, in addition to the ones cited above, mainly time- or space-related words including *tōi* 'far,' *chikai* 'near,' *mae* 'front,' *ushiro* 'behind,' *ima* 'now,' *kinō* 'yesterday,' *koko* 'here,' and *soko* 'there' and the like.

Personal pronouns such as *watakushi* 'I' and *anata* 'you' can also be called "egocentric words." *Watakushi* is a word used by a speaker of Japanese to refer to himself, but when a second speaker starts talking, he calls the first speaker *anata* and refers to himself as *watakushi*.

In the same sense, all kinship terms are egocentric words. For example, imagine a man standing before us. He is a father to his children, a husband to his wife, and a son to his father. Thus, the same person is referred to differently by different relatives, depending on their relationship to him. Consequently, the wider the family circle, the greater the variety of kinship terms applicable to one person.

I have discussed kinship terms as egocentric words in some detail for the following reason. Kinship terms in Japanese dialogues are frequently used not as egocentric words, but in a very special way, which in my view constitutes a marked characteristic of present-day Japanese. This special use of kinship terms corresponds, in my opinion, to a distinctive Japanese behavioral pattern.

Let us listen to a Japanese housewife complaining to her children about her husband coming home late for dinner. *Papa osoi wa ne. Dō shita no kashira* 'Papa is late, isn't he? I wonder what's happened.' I have already pointed out that there is nothing unusual about children saying "Papa is late, isn't he?" but that it is odd for their mother to say the same thing. Since *Papa* is a kinship term meaning "father," a wife saying "Papa is late" should, logically speaking, be referring to her own father, that is, her children's grandfather. However, in Japan, the housewife's utterance would never be misunderstood. For one thing, it is considered such a normal use of the term *Papa* that nobody would ever think twice about who the referent is.

When I described this Japanese phenomenon to Turkish sociologist Niyazi Berkes at McGill University in Canada, who taught me Turkish, he exaggerated his surprise by saying, "A woman's husband is at the same time her papa? That's incest!" He told me that this type of utterance could not occur in Turkish. What then does a Turkish wife call her husband when talking to her children? She says, for example, "Your papa is late, isn't he?" The Turkish word for father is *baba*. To this word is attached the possessive suffix *n* meaning "your." So a Turkish wife talking to her children about her husband always calls him *baban*. What she means is "I'm talking about Papa, but he is your papa, not mine." Thus, in Turkish, whenever one uses a kinship term from another family member's viewpoint, one must specify "whose" relative one is talking about.[13]

Can we then assume from the Turkish example that in Japanese the word meaning "your" is left out but understood? This interpretation, no matter how plausible it may sound, does not really satisfy the linguistic intuition of a native speaker of Japanese. This becomes even more evident when one considers the following example.

One day, when the train I was riding arrived at Shinjuku Station, most passengers got off and many seats were left vacant. At the same time, a wave of new passengers rushed in. Among them was an old lady who walked hurriedly to the seat next to me. As soon as she sat down, she called out, *Mama, koko ni irasshai*, lit., 'Mama, come here!' patting the seat beside her with her hand. Out of the crowd a young woman who had a baby in her arms appeared and sat down next to the old lady. Obviously, it was the woman's daughter who was being called "Mama."

In the direct vocative use of an address term, we cannot possibly explain it away by saying "X's Mama" was abbreviated to mere "Mama." In the light of these examples, it is only natural that Professor Berkes should feel that the Japanese language, which allows one to call one's husband "Papa" and one's daughter "Mama," is crazy. I could cite almost any number of additional examples of this puzzling fictive use of kinship terms among Japanese family members, and they would all be familiar to speakers of Japanese.

I have suggested elsewhere that this type of fictive use be interpreted as follows.[14] A Japanese wife can call her husband *Papa* or *Otōsan* 'Father' when speaking to her children because she is psychologically identifying with them. In other words, the individual who cannot be anything other than her husband from her own standpoint is viewed from her children's perspective. When she uses the egocentric word *Papa*, she mentally transfers the speaker position from herself to her children. What is significant in this case is the fact that she empathizes with her children and identifies with their position. This act of moving closer to one's children's position or perspective is what I call "empathetic identification."

The above phenomenon, however, is not so exceptional that no other examples can be found. For instance, when a gym teacher calls out commands to his students, exactly the same kind of empathetic identification takes place. If the

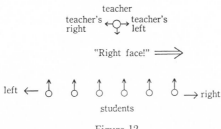

teacher

teacher's right ←○→ teacher's left

"Right face!" ⟹

left ← ○ ○ ○ ○ ○ ○ → right

students

Figure 12

teacher is facing a single line of students as in figure 12, he will call out *Migi muke migi!* 'Right face!' to have them turn to his left. What he calls *migi* 'right' in this case is not the usual egocentric word *migi*, which assumes the speaker's orientation as primary; instead, the teacher means the students' *migi* as he identifies with them and thinks from their viewpoint. A new teacher, unused to this, might inadvertently take himself as the focus and make the mistake of calling out *Hidari muke hidari!* 'Left face!' thus turning his students in the wrong direction.

The use of egocentric words with someone other than oneself as the focal point, but without clearly indicating that this is what is intended, I call an "allocentric use." More strictly, when one clearly verbalizes who the focal point is to be, as in *omae no ushiro* 'your left' or *anata no ushiro* 'behind you,' the allocentric use of words is more proper and clear. However, Japanese kinship terms, as used within the family, often represent the allocentric use. That is why they appear peculiar to speakers of Turkish, in whose language kinship terms do not function in the same way.

The allocentric use of kinship terms, however, is not restricted to Japanese. It can be observed in English, too, although on a more limited scale. For example, in English, a mother speaking to her small child refers to her husband (the child's father) as "Daddy." This, however, is a type of baby talk and is socially recognized as such. In this sense, English is different from Japanese.

My earlier reference to an old woman calling her daughter "Mama" is also an example of empathetic identification. Instead of giving her daughter a linguistic designation directly from her own standpoint, the old woman temporarily identified with the baby the younger woman was carrying, that is, her grandchild. This old lady, by calling this person (her daughter) "Mama," was transferring the speaker focus from herself to the baby.

Many Japanese mothers make a habit of calling their oldest son or daughter *Onīchan* 'Big Brother' or *Onēchan* 'Big Sister.' Structurally, this is exactly the same phenomenon. In this case, the mother tries to view her oldest child not directly from her own standpoint, but indirectly from a younger child's standpoint. Since the younger brother or sister calls the older child by a term denoting 'older brother' or 'older sister,' the mother follows suit by calling the latter *Onīchan* or *Onēchan*.

After examining many examples of this sort, I came to recognize certain patterns in this use of kinship terms.

(1) In the Japanese family, an older member may address a younger member, using the kinship term designating the latter's position from the viewpoint of the youngest member of the family.

(2) When an older family member, in a dialogue with a younger member, mentions a third member who is older than the latter, he does not view this person linguistically

from his own standpoint, but from the standpoint of the hearer, that is, the younger member.

As an example of this second pattern, let me cite a passage from Fumiko Enchi's novel *Onnazaka*, in which the heroine, Rin Shirakawa, refers to her husband as *Ojisama* 'Uncle,' in a dialogue with her nephew, who works as her husband's secretary:

> Thank you very much. I feel so relaxed these days because you can prepare all these papers for us. I am a woman, so I can't handle documents like this, and *Ojisama* [Mr. Shirakawa, her husband] hates bothersome things of this sort.

In every Japanese family, when the father talks to his children about his own father, i.e., their grandfather, he views the latter from the children's standpoint and calls him *Ojisan* 'Grandfather' instead of *Otōsan* 'Father' or *Papa*. On the other hand, when the father talks to his oldest daughter about her younger brother (his own son), he may not call him *Otōto-chan* 'Younger Brother + diminutive marker,' viewing him from her standpoint. Rather, he must view the son directly from his own position. Since, however, a father cannot refer to his son as *Musuko* 'Son' or *Segare* 'Son,' as explained above in rule (2) for the primary use of kinship terms, he ends up using the latter's given name.

To summarize, the outstanding characteristic of what I call the secondary fictive use of Japanese kinship terms is as follows: kinship terms used by an older family member in a dialogue with a younger member are in the final analysis based on the adoption of the youngest member's perspective. Both the person addressed and the person re-

145

ferred to are represented by the terms that show their positions in the family as seen by the youngest member.

Once this principle is understood, it becomes easy to see why young couples in Japan these days often call their only son or their youngest son by the first-person pronoun *boku* 'I.' They sometimes even call him *boku-chan*, adding the diminutive suffix *-chan*, as though *boku* were a given name. For example, a mother might say to her son, *Boku, hayaku irasshai*, lit., 'Me, come here quickly' or *Boku-chan kore hoshii n deshō*, lit., 'Me + dim. wants this, I suppose?' When she speaks in this way, she is thinking of the boy as he would be called if viewed from the position of the youngest member of the family, in this case the boy himself. The boy would naturally call himself *boku*. Therefore, by identifying with him, adults in the family can call him *boku* as well.

Earlier, I mentioned briefly that in a particular social context Japanese people often call unrelated children *Onī- chan* 'Big Brother' or *Onēchan* 'Big Sister.' That also can happen because the speaker, instead of thinking of the addressee directly from his own position, tentatively assumes the latter to have a younger brother or sister and then identifies with this imaginary person. If the addressee is a very little boy, the personal pronoun *boku* is sometimes used. That, too, can be explained similarly: the speaker is viewing the little boy from the latter's position by assuming him to be the youngest member of an imaginary family. That is how the speaker comes to call the little boy *boku*, allocentrically using an address term which is primarily an egocentric term for self.

This method of linguistically designating an addressee from the standpoint of someone who is not present or who may not even exist is more prevalent in people's linguistic behavior than is generally assumed. In an article coauthored by two American sociologists, Homans and Schneider,[15] they reported that one of them was walking past a new suburban apartment complex one day when he saw a little boy of about four having trouble with an untied shoelace. This child looked up at him and shouted, "Somebody's Daddy! Please fix my shoelace!" The authors say that in an apartment complex of this sort, each family has one or more children. To these children, therefore, neighborhood adults are always "X's father" or "Y's mother," because they are used to identifying these adults in their minds indirectly, in relation to their own playmates. The authors contend that when an unfamiliar adult walked by, this particular child first established in his mind a playmate, X, who could serve as the point of reference, and then addressed the man as the imaginary playmate's father. Hence the expression "Somebody's Daddy."

From Truk Island in the South Pacific, another interesting example is reported.[16] On that island, when the first child of a man called A is born, it is predetermined that the child will be named B. When B has children, the first one is to be given the name C. In this way, a limited number of names are used in a circular fashion, repeating themselves in a few generations. In anthropology, these are called "cyclic names." Truk islanders customarily avoid the use of real names, so that they do not address one another by name. Instead they call A "B's father," and B "C's father," and so on. Even an unmarried child is addressed in exactly the same fashion. This is possible because what his or her child's name is going to be is already known to everyone through the system of cyclic names. In other words, one is given a linguistic designation in relation to someone yet unborn.

Misao Tōjō's *Zenkoku hōgen jiten* [National dialect dictionary] lists a dialectal use of *oji* 'uncle' in the sense of "a younger brother; a second son or younger." Likewise, under *oba* 'aunt,' there is a listing of "a younger sister; a second daughter or younger." Since these listings are so simple, it is not clear under what circumstances these words can carry these meanings. According to my own observations in Awa County, Chiba Prefecture, people there say "Such-and-such is an *oji* (or *oba*) of the X family." I am a third son myself, and was once called *Oji* by an inhabitant there.

I brought up this dialectal use of *oji* and *oba* because I feel that this practice too can be explained by pointing out that structurally it is the same as other examples above. It is an instance of denoting someone on the basis of his position within the family as seen from a person not present or still unborn. Under the old constitution, the oldest son of a Japanese family was destined to succeed to the father's position to lead the main branch of the family. In those days, when the main family was considered to set a standard for all relatives, sons and daughters who were not the oldest were the ones to be called eventually *Oji* 'Uncle' or *Oba* 'Aunt' by the oldest son's children. Therefore, in my opinion, even someone outside the family can call these sons and daughters *Oji* or *Oba* by identifying with the oldest son's present or future children. My supposition cannot be verified due to the paucity of data, but the fact that this usage is found centered in the Tōhoku and Kantō regions (northeast Honshū) seems to support my view at least tentatively.†

†These are the regions where primogeniture was prevalent.

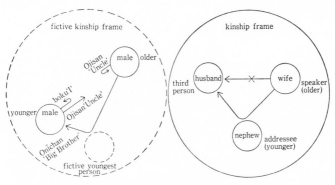

Figure 13

Insofar as assuming a hypothetical person's existence is concerned, the examples cited above from English and from Truk Island have something in common with the second fictive use of Japanese kinship terms. However, when it comes to the way the kinship terms are used, there is a clearcut difference.

In the English example, the fact that this *Daddy* is not the speaker's father is clearly signaled by *somebody's*, which modifies *Daddy*. This is structurally the same as the utterance of the Turkish mother who, in dialogue with her child, always calls the child's father *baban* 'your father.' The Truk Islanders' use of "B's father," too, is structurally the same.

In the case of Japanese, on the other hand, the speaker completely identifies himself with the imaginary or absent party, from whose viewpoint he then refers to the addressee. As a result, the speaker simply needs to call the hearer *Oni-chan* 'Big Brother' and himself *Ojisan* 'Uncle' without indicating whose brother or uncle each is.

Language and Patterns of Behavior

So far I have presented an overview of the terms used by a speaker of present-day Japanese to refer to himself and his addressee. Such an interesting area of sociolinguistics has been so neglected that it has not been described in detail or examined systematically, probably because of the commonplace nature of the phenomenon. However, I do not think that is the sole reason. No study of Japanese from this angle has been conducted because this problem does not arise within the framework of Western linguistics, which has served as the model for modern linguistics in Japan. In fact, Western linguistics has never found it necessary to deal with problems of this sort because such phenomena do not exist in Occidental languages.

Japanese linguists have only looked for topics in Japanese which are the same as, or similar to, the ones already treated in Western linguistics, and thus they have discussed the differences between Japanese and Western languages while weighing the values of phenomena in the former by criteria applicable to the latter. Nevertheless, once we discard this attitude, we suddenly notice many interesting topics that are left untouched.

For example, let us return to the question of terms that are used for the addressee. In Japan, when parents scold children, they call them by their first names, as in *Tarō, yame-nasai* 'Tarō, cut it out!' In English, on the other hand, if parents or teachers are really angry, they might use not only the child's first name, but his last name also,[17] as in "George Franklin, cut it out!" If the child has a middle name, that might also be added. Japanese parents, however, would never scold their children, saying things like *Yama-moto Tarō, yame-nasai* 'Tarō Yamamoto, cut it out!" How do we account for this difference?

If we pursue the topic of terms of self-reference further, we come to the question of how a Japanese addresses himself while speaking to himself. English speakers often call themselves "you," referring to themselves in the second person.[18] Furthermore, in many cases, they begin by calling themselves by name. "Miss [Jane] Marple sighed, then admonished herself in words, though she did not speak those words aloud. 'Now, Jane, what are you suggesting or thinking?' " Would a Japanese named Tarō ever say to himself "Now, Tarō, what are you thinking?" in Japanese? Answering a question like this is far from simple. Moreover, we cannot look to European grammars or language studies for guides, for there are none. An issue like this only arises when one compares Japanese with English from new angles.

In closing I would like to put forward one or two theories of my own as to how the unique structure of Japanese terms of self-reference and address relates to the characteristic patterns of behavior and thought of the Japanese.

Japanese terms of self-reference and address may be construed as serving to specify and confirm the concrete roles of the speaker and the addressee. "Role" may be defined here as a concept referring to a specific pattern of behavior which an individual with specific qualifications and qualities generally demonstrates within a given social context. For example, military men, teachers, and policemen naturally behave in accordance with their occupations and are expected by others to behave in that way. Old people and children exhibit different patterns of behavior for various

151

reasons and can therefore be said to play different roles. There are obviously a very great number of roles in society.

Among these roles, there are some which continue for a relatively long time, for example, inherent roles as males or females, social roles based on class differences in a stratified society, occupational roles, and roles as parents or children within the family. On the other hand, there are various roles which last for a relatively short time, for example, those based on the relationship between sales clerk and customer, between passengers on the same train, between speaker and addressee, and so on.

If we introduce this concept of role into the question of how a speaker of Japanese conceives of himself and the addressee linguistically, the structural difference between Japanese and other languages, especially European languages, becomes evident.

In such languages as Latin and English, the speaker first of all expresses himself by means of a first-person pronoun and then calls the addressee by a second-person pronoun. However, when he stops talking, the other person takes over and uses a first-person pronoun for himself. The person who spoke first naturally is the addressee now and is referred to by a second-person pronoun.

This switching back and forth between first-person and second-person pronouns can be considered natural when one accepts the following: a first-person pronoun is nothing but a word whereby the user signals that he is the one speaking now, a word by which he demonstrates his momentary role. A second-person pronoun, on the other hand, is a word with which the speaker indicates to the addressee, "You are the hearer now."

First- and second-person pronouns in the Indo-European languages have nothing to do with the concrete properties (position, age, sex, etc.) that the speaker or the addressee possesses. They merely serve the function of signaling abstract linguistic roles, the role of an active agent and that of a passive agent, in a language activity called a dialogue. These pronouns are exactly like the masks worn by Nō actors to indicate their respective roles. When an actor plays a different role, which he may do within a single play, he only has to change the mask. Personal pronouns in European languages are "personal" because they are originally words with the characteristics of *persona*, i.e., masks used in classical plays.

The exchange of *ego/tu* in Latin and *I/you* in English thus linguistically represents human relations that are symmetrical. It is true that many European languages such as French and German have been using two kinds of second-person pronouns since the beginning of the Modern Ages, and have therefore drifted away slightly from the original pattern described above. Even so, the fact that personal pronouns originally started out with the function described here is not to be denied.

If we examine Japanese dialogues from this role-related viewpoint, what do we discover? Let us take the case of a father and son as an example. A father generally calls himself *Papa* or *Otōsan* 'Father' when talking to his son. He calls his son sometimes *omae* 'you,' and sometimes by name. The son may call the father *Papa* or *Otōsan*, but cannot use personal pronouns or the latter's name. As for terms for self, the son uses *boku* 'I' or, more rarely, his own name. From this we can see clearly that the use of terms of self-reference and terms of address in Japanese is, as a rule, asymmetrical.

Now, when a father calls himself *Papa*, he is actually confirming his role as a parent to his son, the addressee, through language. This in turn assigns to the other, though indirectly and implicitly, a dependent role as his child, for the concept of father exists only in opposition to the concept of child. A father may call himself "Father" only when talking to his children.

Likewise, the act of a son calling his father *Papa* implies the confirmation of two types of roles. First, directly and explicitly, he designates and confirms the addressee's role as a father. Second, by calling the addressee *Papa*, the son expresses indirectly and implicitly his willingness to accept his

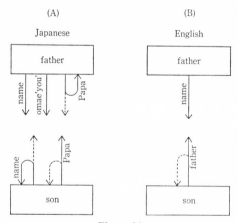

Figure 14

The broken lines indicate the indirect, implicit confirmation or assignment of roles; the solid arrows signify the direct, explicit confirmation or assignment of roles.

role as a son of the addressee, for to be able to call a certain person *Papa*, one has to be his child.

Furthermore, in a dialogue between father and son, if the father calls the son by his name, he is indicating that he has assumed the role of a superior in his relationship with his son. Likewise, the fact that the father may call the son by a personal pronoun (not vice versa) strengthens his confirmed role as a superior. Figure 14 shows this relationship.

In other words, when a father talks to his son, the confirmation of his role as a superior is constantly repeated from his side in three direct-explicit ways and one indirect-implicit way, therefore in four different ways all together. From the son's side, his role as an inferior is confirmed verbally in two direct ways and two indirect ways, therefore in four ways in all. That is to say, in a dialogue between these two people, the mutual designation and confirmation of roles are carried out in eight different ways. And of course, the terms used between father and son are not limited to those cited above, I have merely cited the ones directly related to the confirmation of roles for the sake of simplicity.

Let us next consider the case of an English-speaking father and son. Unlike their Japanese counterparts, they almost always conduct their dialogues, as mentioned earlier, by means of a symmetrical exchange of *I* and *you*. As far as confirming each other's role as father or son is concerned, the only exceptions to symmetry are the father calling the son by name and the son calling the father "Father," "Daddy," "Dad," etc.

The confirmation by the son of the father's role by calling him "Father" has two meanings, direct and indirect, as is the case with Japanese. However, English differs from Japanese in that under some unusual circumstances the father may call his son "Son" or "Sonny." This occurs, for example, when the father is particularly conscious of his family ties with his son or when he feels his love for his son more acutely than usual. But this usage is far more restricted than "Father," which a son often uses in addressing his father. The practice of the father calling his son by name but not vice versa is the same as in Japanese. This serves as the father's explicit and direct confirmation of his own role as a superior.

Thus, in father-son relations in an English-speaking society there are normally three ways of confirming each other's role by means of words: two ways, direct and indirect, from the son's side and one direct way from the father's side. Two more ways may be added when the father addresses the son as "Son."

Now, when one compares this with Japanese, in which eight different ways of role confirmation constantly take place, one must realize how much importance the Japanese attach to roles based on superior-inferior oppositions in everyday human relationships.

Of course, designating or confirming roles can also be done by means other than language; one must therefore realize that linguistic differences do not necessarily represent differences between English speakers and Japanese speakers in their respective ways of viewing the roles of individuals in social life as a whole. Nevertheless, since language activities are clearly articulated and more explicit in nature than other types of activities, whether or not speakers of a specific language constantly confirm each other's roles verbally in every human relationship should certainly indicate a considerable difference. Whereas speakers of European languages can usually carry on a dialogue by merely indicating the abstract roles of the speaker and the addressee, in Japanese all terms for self-reference and for address are connected with the confirmation of concrete roles based on a superior-inferior dichotomy in human relationships.[19]

The various qualities and attributes we humans possess may be classified into two general types. One is the inherent type, e.g., age, sex, and station in a stratified society. These are not consciously acquired and do not allow the person concerned any free choice. The other is the type which one acquires on one's own; their acquisition is based on free choices made by the person concerned. In terms of human relations, blood ties are inherent, whereas relations based on promises and contracts are acquired.

However, which of the two categories described above is recognized as being of greater value is determined by the structure of one's culture and society. In Japan, where practices such as permanent employment, a seniority system of promotions, and male predominance are still common, society places more value on inherent qualifications. Japanese society is therefore often contrasted to American society, for example, where both one's abilities and occupation as well as one's degree of wealth are regarded as acquired.

In actuality, however, whether a characteristic is inherent or acquired is, with the exception of things like sex and age which can be objectively verified, often based on the interpretation of the people in a given society. That is, whether to classify a particular person's attributes or state in one category or another is not clear until we know what provides the frames of reference of the particular culture.

I would now like to examine a few linguistic facts in order

to determine which the Japanese consider more important
—roles relating to inherent properties or roles based on
acquired conditions.

In Japan today, the majority of husbands and wives call
each other *Papa/Mama* or *Otōsan/Okāsan* 'Father/Mother.'
But there are also many couples who say that they used to
call each other by name when they were newlyweds. It
is very common for a husband to call his wife by name
while she addresses him with a pronoun only, such as *anata*
'you.' Nevertheless, as soon as such couples have a child,
most of them start calling each other *Papa/Mama* or *Otōsan/
Okāsan*. How do we account for this?

At the time a man and a woman are married, they may be
regarded as having entered a relationship based on a kind
of contract. Both the role of husband and that of wife have
to be played semiconsciously, since they are roles actively
chosen and entered into by these people. Consequently, the
state of marriage in which the husband and wife find themselves, alone as a couple until the first child is born, contains
a certain degree of insecurity akin to tension.

Upon the arrival of a child, the husband becomes a father,
and the wife a mother. The role of a father or a mother is
not a chosen role which one has to play consciously, but
rather a natural one. Once a person becomes a father, he
cannot easily annul that role. The parent-child relationship,
since it allows no room for free choice, provides a greater
sense of security, at least for the Japanese, than does the
husband-wife relationship. The husband and wife therefore
try to enter a more permanent and secure state by convert-
ing their original horizontal relationship to a vertical relationship based on the child whom they share, that is, the

natural relationship in which both are parents of the same child. This search for security may be behind the common switch to address terms denoting "father" and "mother."

If this interpretation is correct, Japanese couples act more frequently as their children's parents than as each other's husband or wife. In fact, it is my view that Japanese couples do behave in that way when compared with couples in other countries, especially the United States.

It is generally accepted that Americans place more value on acquired roles than on assigned roles, or roles which one does not choose freely. This applies to marital and parental roles, among others. Indeed, in the eyes of the Japanese, American couples act as husband and wife to a surprising degree. Marriage in America begins first of all with the exchange of rings, which symbolize mutual restriction. A great deal of effort is constantly made to maintain the marriage. Exchanging words of love is common, as is the exchange of gifts on wedding anniversaries and birthdays. These overt manifestations of affection are nothing but rituals serving to reconfirm and strengthen the contractual state called marriage. Since marriage is a contractual state, forgetting or slackening the observance of these overt expressions of love might immediately lead marriage to failure.

Japanese couples, on the other hand, hardly ever express love overtly, nor do they use socially formalized terms such as English *honey* and *darling*, which social anthropologists call "saccharine terms." This probably indicates that, for the Japanese, marriage is not a dynamic, direct, contractual relationship, which the persons concerned must maintain by constant confirmation of their love for one another. For them, it is rather a natural, noncontractual relationship, based on the static and unchangeable parent-child relationship, which theoretically can be neither denied nor annulled.

With reference to roles, there is another notable pattern of behavior peculiar to the Japanese, which is closely related to the Japanese self-definition dependent on the addressee, a topic to be discussed in the next section. This is the strong aversion to dealing simultaneously with two or more people of mutually exclusive roles or vastly different statuses that might require completely opposite responses.

At the height of the campus disorder in Japan (1960s), university professors were in a reflective mood. We even went as far as discussing means of improving the instructional efforts, though not necessarily the research efforts, of university professors. At one meeting, I once suggested a plan to encourage the faculty of my institution to attend each other's classes. My reason for suggesting this was that we faculty members tend to become self-centered and conceited in terms of both teaching and knowledge. Attending the lectures of colleagues should teach us a great deal. Having colleagues attend our classes should also give us a chance to let them know more about us. All in all, I believed this would be a desirable goal.

An extremely interesting and unexpected objection was raised: when we teach in the classroom, we assume the role of educators dealing with students. If a colleague or a senior member of the staff were to appear in our class, we would probably try so hard to impress the visitor that our lecture would turn into something like a paper read at a professional conference. That would be undesirable from an educational point of view. Hearing this opinion, I was again impressed by a cultural difference between Japan and other countries, for I have often observed at American and Canadian universities that any faculty member, when asked by colleagues for permission to attend his lectures, invariably expresses happiness and considers the presence of a colleague in his class an honor.

Generally speaking, in North America, once a colleague is permitted to attend a class, the instructor in charge of the class treats him as a student, regardless of age or seniority. In a seminar, he asks the colleague questions and calls on him to do the same work as any other student. Since they do not bring their social positions or their relationship from outside the class into the classroom, the professor and his colleague fit into the contractual teacher-student relationship without difficulty. The visitor, who is treated like a student, does not feel too shy to ask questions or to enter a discussion. This, however, does not happen in Japan. The instructor here would find it difficult to teach well.

It is not only colleagues, in fact, who would cause problems for an instructor. The presence of a member of his family, such as his child or wife, would also affect the instructor adversely. Teachers who ask someone else to take over their courses, feeling uncomfortable about facing their own children in class, are not exceptional in Japan.

At American universities, on the other hand, there are often not only children attending their parents' classes, but sometimes even wives taking their husbands' courses as students. A Japanese husband would not hear of it. In Japan, relationships between *senpai* (senior) and *kōhai* (junior), between colleagues, parent and child, husband and wife, etc., require the participants to play fixed roles, which should not vary even with a change in time or place.

161

When A and B are husband and wife, their relationship cannot easily be switched to a teacher-student relationship. For the same reason, if a senior member of the faculty is sitting with the students in class, the instructor in charge loses his secure ground, for his role and self-definition vis-à-vis the senior member collide with those vis-à-vis the students. In linguistic terms, for example, there is the problem of whether to refer to himself as *boku* 'I' or *watakushi* 'I.'†

The presence of an instructor's wife among the students would complicate the issue even more. Generally speaking, the husband-wife relationship in Japan is an extremely private one. In public, couples try not to make an ostentatious display of their relationship; in fact, they often behave towards each other as though they were unrelated. Therefore, even nowadays, some husbands hate their wives visiting or telephoning them at their place of work. They feel that their relationships with their wives and their relationships with other people at work belong to different and mutually exclusive levels. In short, for most Japanese, a relationship between two specific persons is intrinsically a fixed one involving only two roles, e.g., husband and wife, or teacher and student.

A relationship between two Americans, on the other hand, is much more flexible, allowing a far greater variety of roles. This is why husband and wife can be at the same time teacher and student, friends, or even rivals.

When American graduate students earn their doctorates,

†Many male speakers of Japanese feel that when they address superiors, they should refer to themselves as *watakushi*, a more formal term than *boku*.

they soon start calling their former professors by their first names. The reason is that in the United States the concept of colleagueship is an egalitarian one and supersedes differences in seniority, scholarship, or age. In contrast, I still cannot call an old professor from my university days by any term other than *Sensei* 'Teacher.' This is more than twenty years after graduation. The fact that specific Japanese interpersonal pairs are fixed in terms of the role of each member and are virtually immune to changes of situation and passage of time cannot be unrelated to the extremely concrete structure of the linguistic designations we use to address one another in Japanese.

The use of terms for self-reference such as *watakushi* and *boku* can be interpreted as the speaker's act of identifying his status or role linguistically. In Indo-European languages, in Turkish, and in Arabic, terms for self—those by which the speaker refers to himself—are in fact almost exclusively limited to first-person pronouns. The function of these pronouns is, briefly stated, to designate the user explicitly as the speaker. The meaning of the act of using *ego* in Latin or *I* in English is to express verbally that the one who is speaking at this moment is nobody else but me. No other information concerning the speaker is contained in these pronouns.

This type of self-appellation has the following characteristic. Linguistic self-designation by the speaker takes place spontaneously and independently of the hearer or the surrounding circumstances. It can and does take place even without a hearer present. To be precise, the speaker's linguistic self-recognition precedes his recognition of the other's presence. That is to say, only after the speaker first confirms himself as the active participant in a speech act and chooses *ego* (or *I*), can the addressee, the passive participant, be linguistically designated as *tu* (or *you*) in opposition to *ego* (or *I*). The order of recognition is therefore *ego→tu* (or *I→you* in English).

In Japanese, on the other hand, I conclude from the structure of terms for self which I have described in this chapter that the order is exactly reversed. Let us, for example, consider someone who calls himself *Papa* at home. In order for him to be able to designate himself as *Papa*, he must first of all have a child and then recognize the fact that he is talking to that child. He cannot designate himself as *Papa* unless he identifies himself with the child who is face to face with him. To outsiders, he is not *Papa* at all. Therefore, in this case, his choice of a term of self-designation is obviously based on the presence of a specific addressee. This is exactly what I mean when I say that, unlike European languages, designation of the other (the addressee) precedes self-designation in Japanese. The fact that the Japanese elementary school teacher may call himself *Sensei* 'Teacher' only when talking to his students can be explained in exactly the same way. Furthermore, our fictive use of such terms as *Onēsan* 'Big Sister' and *Ojisan* 'Uncle' to refer to ourselves when talking to a child who is a stranger is also based on our supposition as to what relative we would correspond to from the child's point of view. This is precisely why I contend that self-designation in Japanese is relative and other-oriented in comparison with the absolute type of self-designation in Indo-European languages, which allows one to designate oneself first of all as a speaker, an active user of language, regardless of who the addressee is or whether or not there is an addressee.

164

This applies even to the Japanese speaker's use of the so-called first-person pronouns. For instance, adult males distinguish between *watakushi* and *boku*, or *boku* and *ore*, depending on the occasion and the addressee. This discriminating use of first-person pronouns is said to reflect the difference in power between the speaker and the addressee as well as the degree of familiarity between the two, but this too falls under other-oriented self-designation inasmuch as it is dependent on a specific addressee each time. Thus the Japanese ego may be construed as being in an indefinite state, with its position undetermined, until a specific addressee, a concrete person, appears and is identified by the speaker.

The other-oriented structure of self-designation in Japanese is obviously related to another behavior pattern of ours: our reluctance to engage in casual conversations with strangers. If we cannot identify the other person relative to ourselves, we cannot establish a proper relationship with him. Consequently, the speaker is left in an insecure and indefinite state and cannot easily form a secure relationship with the other.

Those whose identities are the least clear to the Japanese are foreigners. Since we Japanese have grown up in a homogeneous society, we cannot gather enough information merely by looking at a foreigner to determine who he is. One might say that our ability to identify the other suffers a kind of paralysis due to the shock of seeing a "red-haired, blue-eyed" person.

Father Grootaers, a Belgian priest who has been living in Tokyo for many years, is a linguist with an excellent command of Japanese. He once coauthored a highly informative book called *Goyaku*.[20] In it is a passage relevant to my point. At a bakery in his neighborhood which he passes almost daily, Father Grootaers is always understood perfectly when he says *Shokupan ikkin kudasai* 'I would like a loaf of bread, please,' but at a downtown bakery he sometimes has difficulty making himself understood even though he uses the same sentence and pronounces it exactly the same way. Furthermore, when he travels through the countryside, he has great difficulty communicating with people just because he looks different. Sometimes people he talks to refuse to recognize that he is addressing them in Japanese. They just keep repeating *Watashi eigo wakarimasen* 'I don't understand English,' moving an open hand back and forth before their faces to emphasize their negative response, disregarding his very fluent Japanese.

I recently came across a very interesting article in a magazine called *Gengo seikatsu* on the mental block which most Japanese experience toward foreigners.[21] It reported the results of a survey conducted by Makoto Takada of the National Language Research Institute attempting to determine the level of proficiency of average Tokyoites in spoken English. For this survey, he went around Tokyo with an American T. E. Huber, a lecturer of English at Nippon University. While Mr. Huber asked passersby some simple English questions which had been prepared in advance, Mr. Takada observed from nearby, pretending to be a mere bystander, and recorded his observations. After interviewing about sixty people at three different locations (Hongō, Ginza, and Shinjuku), they found only a handful who somehow managed to converse in English.

Be that as it may, what really interests me is a comment made by Mr. Takada in his conclusion. Concerning the attitudes of the people who were addressed by Mr. Huber, Mr. Takada writes: "Aside from those who did not bother to stop, those who stopped to answer generally showed a lack of self-confidence. They somehow looked intimidated. Since inability to speak English really is no reflection on one's character, I wished that they would not sneak away, raise their shoulders defiantly, or grin unnecessarily as they did, but that they would instead look Mr. Huber in the face. It was frustrating for me as I observed from the sidelines."

Such behavior as sneaking away, becoming defiant, and grinning are signals of these people's attempts to escape a state of mental insecurity brought on by unexpected contact with the unfamiliar and unplaceable. The overt manifestations can be regarded as a kind of displacement activity in the sense the term is used in ethology.

Other-oriented self-designation is, to put it another way, the assimilation of the self, who is the observer, with the other, who is the observed, with no clear distinction made between the positions of the two. It is frequently pointed out that whereas Western culture is based on the distinction between the observer and the observed, on the opposition of the self versus the other, Japanese culture and sentiment show a strong tendency to overcome this distinction by having the self immerse itself in the other. We have seen elements in the structure of the Japanese language which definitely support this view.

We Japanese are not particularly good at expressing our own opinions and making our positions clear before we have considered the addressee's feelings and thoughts. Rather, we feel comfortable with other-oriented behavior, that is, waiting for the other person to express himself first and then adapting our view accordingly. Moreover, it sometimes even happens that, before the other person states his opinion or wish clearly, we read his mind and adjust our behavior to it. Common expressions such as *sasshi ga yoi* 'good at guessing another's feeling,' *ki ga kiku* 'quick to read another's mind,' and *omoiyari ga aru* 'considerate of others' feelings' are all words of praise difficult to translate literally into European languages, a further indication that self-assimilation with the other is a virtue among the Japanese.

Such expressions as *shinsetsu no oshiuri* 'forcing kindness on others,' *arigata-meiwaku* 'annoyance caused by someone's unwelcome kindness,' *Hito no ki mo shiranai de ii ki na mono da* 'He is happy not knowing how I feel' (a critical remark) make sense in Japan because it is a society in which the common practice is to try to guess others' feelings and wishes before they are verbally expressed. This also explains why the Japanese themselves call their culture *sasshi no bunka*, lit., 'guessing culture' and *omoiyari no bunka*, lit., 'consideration culture.' Because it is considered essential to identify with the other and feel as he feels, a free exchange of opposing views between individuals is restrained to the utmost. Likewise, the function of language as a regulator of the interests of both parties is also suppressed. This type of "considerate" communication may at its worst slide from trying to read another's thoughts and feelings to becoming ill under the burden of another's worries. But at the same time it contains the possibility of being elevated to the philosophy of the tea ceremony: "Boundless consideration towards guests."

The mentality of assimilating oneself with the other recognizes the value in voluntarily overcoming the distinction between the self and the other. This is again related to the rather unique mental climate in Japan which is described by psychiatrist Takeo Doi as *amae* 'dependence psychology.' What makes such blending of individuals possible is Japan's extreme homogeneity in culture, race, and religion, but this has already been pointed out by others, so I will not deal with the topic again here.

I should, however, like to add one more thing before closing. As long as Japanese deal with one another inside Japan, such Japanese traits as dependence and the assimilation of oneself with the other function well as they are and do not pose serious problems. But these characteristics lose their effectiveness as soon as we start dealing with non-Japanese.

We Japanese are used to identifying with, and depending on, one another. Without thinking twice, we project ourselves on others and become dependent on them. At the same time we expect them to adjust to us. We often fail to realize that it is impossible for us to be understood by non-Japanese without expressing ourselves clearly. Furthermore, we are poor at establishing our own views and positions until we know where the other person stands. This leaves our dealings with other countries continually one step behind in such areas as diplomacy and politics. We just cannot place ourselves until we grasp the general situation.

Japanese are mostly poor speakers of foreign languages and, as a result, suffer unreasonably at international conferences despite their potential for making contributions. But, in my opinion, this should not be explained as lack of language aptitude alone. It may be in large part due to our lack of determination to express ourselves fully in words, and particularly our lack of self-assertiveness in presenting our opinion no matter what others may say or feel.[22]

Notes

Chapter 1

1. Jowett, B., *The Dialogues of Plato*, Vol. 1 (Oxford: Clarendon Press, 1953).
2. Suzuki, Takao, "Nihon no gaikokugo kenkyū ni kakete-ita mono" [What has been lacking in foreign-language research in Japan], *Gogaku kyoiku*, No. 291, IRLT, 1970.
3. The following quotation is an example of this proverb used to refer to a series of desirable events: "As a matter of fact I went to Hurst Park. Backed two winners. It never rains but it pours! If your luck's in, it's in!" (Agatha Christie, *After the Funeral*)
4. Suzuki, Takao, *op. cit.*

Chapter 2

1. Suzuki, Takao, "*Tengu* no hana wa naze takai" [Why is the *tengu*'s nose high?], *Gengo seikatsu*, No. 191, August, 1967.

Chapter 3

1. Actually the Japanese word *akai* 'red' is not without problems. For example, men's *akagutsu*, lit., 'red shoes,' are not really red. See Suzuki, Takao, "Shikisaigo no imi-bunseki ni kansuru ichi-kōsatsu" [Semantic analysis

of color words], *Keiōgijuku daigaku gengo bunka kenkyūjo kiyō*, No. 4, December, 1974.

2. Leisi, Ernst, *Der Wortinhalt: Seine Struktur im deutschen und englischen*, 2, Erweiterte Auflage (Heidelberg: Quelle & Meyer, 1961).

3. Suzuki, Takao, "An Essay on the Anthropomorphic Norm," in Jakobson, Roman and Kawamoto, Shigeo (eds.), *Studies in General and Oriental Linguistics* (Tokyo: TEC, 1970).

Chapter 4

1. This distinction between "meaning" and "definition" was first outlined in Suzuki, Takao, "Kotoba no imi" [Meanings of words] in Morioka, Kenji; Nagano, Ken; and Miyaji, Yutaka (eds.), *Vocabulary*, Vol. 4, *Kōza: Tadashii Nihongo* [Lectures: Correct Japanese] (Tokyo: Meiji Shoin, 1970).

2. Nishio, Minoru; Iwabuchi, Etsutarō; and Mizutani, Shizuo (eds.), *Iwanami kokugo jiten* [Iwanami Japanese dictionary] (Tokyo: Iwanami, 1963).

3. Except in the case of dyed hair, where this use of *wear* may be possible.

Chapter 5

1. The following excerpt illustrates this practice: "Even before her husband was a prisoner with the Japs all she had for company was a cow, a couple of dozen hens and a terrier that hunted the rats that infested the hen-run. The blow of losing her husband to the Japs was followed by the blow of losing the terrier when it severed a leg in a

gin-trap she had set for hares. She promptly shot the dog with a double-barrelled shot-gun and after that she was quite alone." (H. E. Bates, *The Triple Echo*)

2. It is interesting to note that in recent years people's attitude toward dogs seems to have changed considerably in England and in France too. The number of abandoned dogs is reportedly on the increase in these countries, because many people just leave their dogs behind when they go abroad for the long summer holidays. These same people often keep pets at resorts and abandon them when the summer is over.

   It may be a reflection of this changing attitude toward dogs that the last British naval attache family which resided in the house across from mine turned out to be an exception to the rule. All day long, their dog barked at people passing their house to the great nuisance of their neighbors and behaved so wildly when taken out for a walk that the Captain was obliged to hold it down by grasping its collar whenever they met another dog.

3. I should like to have the reader compare this incident with the one described in the following article, "100 Huskies Killed as Economic Measure," which appeared in the *Times*, April 19, 1975, two years after the first edition of my book was published in Japan.

   A hundred husky dogs were killed by members of the British Antarctic survey as an economy measure it was disclosed yesterday.

   Most were shot when a base at Stonington Island was closed down. Others, mainly puppies, were put to sleep with drug injections, Mr. Graham Wright of Sale, Cheshire, who was in charge of the base, said. He was speaking at Southampton, where the Antarctic survey ship John Biscoe docked yesterday.

The base was closed because the survey is cutting down on dog transport and using motorized vehicles to cut costs, he said.

The huskies were shot by their keepers and buried in a large trench. "It was very distressing. When there are just two of you alone in the field with 18 dogs you can imagine how attached you get to them" Mr. Wright said. Most were shot because it was felt that was the quicket way.

Mr. Erick Salmon, the survey's personnel officer, said: "It is much more economical to do without them. It would have been impractical to have saved them and moved them elsewhere."

4. Over the last ten odd years since this book was written, horses have almost completely been replaced by motorized tractors in Japanese farming. Horse-drawn carts have also become a thing of the past.

5. Leach, Edmund, "Animal Categories and Verbal Abuse," in Lenneberg, E. (ed.), *New Directions in the Study of Language*, (Cambridge, Mass: MIT Press 1966).

6. Suzuki, Takao, *A Semantic Analysis of Present-Day Japanese, with Particular Reference to the Role of Chinese Characters* (Tokyo: Keio University, 1963).

7. Suzuki, Takao, "On'in-kōtai to igi-bunka no kankei ni tsuite—iwayuru seidaku no tairitsu o chūshin to shite"

[On the Relationship Between Phonemic Alteration and Semantic Differentiation with Particular Reference to Voiced vs. Voiceless Sounds] *Gengo-Kenkyū*, No. 42, Tokyo, Nihon Gengo Gakkai, 1963.

8. Suzuki, Takao, "Nihonjin to Nihongo" ('Japanese People and the Japanese Language'), *Gengo*, No. 10, Tokyo, Taishukan, 1973.

Chapter 6

1. Suzuki, Takao, "Gengo to shakai" [Language and society], *Iwanami-kōza tetsugaku* [Iwanami lecture series, philosophy], XI, Ch. 9 (Tokyo: Iwanami Shoten, 1968). Suzuki, Takao, "Nihongo no jishōshi" [Japanese terms for self], *Energy*, No. 17, 1968. Suzuki, Takao, "Jibun oyobi aite o sasu kotoba—gengo shakaigakku no ichi-kadai" [Terms for the speaker and the addressee—a sociolinguistic problem], *Gakujutsu geppō*, XXIII, No. 12, 1971.

2. Suzuki, Takao, "Shinzokumeishō ni yoru eigo no jikohyōgen to koshō—bungaku-sakuhin ni arawareta yōrei o chushin to suru yobi-chōsa" [English kinship terms used as terms for self or address terms—a preliminary survey based on examples from literary works], *Keiōgijuku daigaku gengobunka kenkyūjo kiyō*, no. 1, 1970.

3. *Taishōshi* may be taken as words referring to the addressee, cf. n. 4 below.

4. *Jishō, taishō, tashō* are terms which have been used by Japanese grammarians for some time, but they are in most cases used as substitute labels for *first, second,* and *third person,* respectively, and not in the broader sense that I am using them here.

174

5. Sakuma, Kanae, "Gengo ni okeru suijunten'i—toku ni Nihongo ni okeru jindaimeishi no hensen ni tsuite" [Shifts in levels—particularly concerning the changes in Japanese personal pronouns], 1937, reprinted in his *Nihongo no gengoriron* [Linguistic theories concerning the Japanese language] (Tokyo: Kōseikaku, 1959).

6. Tsujimura, Toshiki, "*Kisama* no hensen" [How *kisama* has changed in status], 1953, reprinted in his *Keigo no shiteki kenkyū* [A historical study of Japanese respect language] (Tokyo: Tokyodo, 1968).

7. Fischer, J. L., "Words for Self and Others in Some Japanese Families," *American Anthropologist*, LXVI, No. 6, Part 2, 1964.

8. Suzuki, Takao, "Gengo to shakai" [Language and Society] *loc. cit.* Watanabe, Tomosuke, "Nihonjin no shinzoku-koshō ni tsuite no jirei-kenkyū, 1" [Survey of samples of Japanese kinship terms, 1], in the second section of Watanabe's *Shakai kōzō to gengo no kankei ni tsuite no kisoteki kenkyū* [Basic study of the relationship between social structure and language] (Tokyo: Kokuritsu Kokugo Kenkyūjo, 1965), reports in detail the kinship terms used in the Jisaku Watanabe family in Hobara-machi, Date County, Fukushima Prefecture. However, the basic principles set down in this report support the validity of the rules I described earlier in "Gengo to shakai."

9. Unlike *seito* 'student [especially through high school age],' *gakusei* 'student [especially college age or above]' can be used with the suffix-*san* as a term of address. This may be because the word *gakusei* does not constitute a pair with a word of the opposite meaning as does

seito, which is paired with *sensei* 'teacher.' *Gakusei* is instead regarded as the name of an occupation or a social position.

10. In English, too, there is an interesting practice of doctors, nurses, and teachers which calls for the use of *we* instead of *you* when addressing someone. They use *we* when they as guardians feel psychologically superior to the addressee. For more on this point, see Suzuki, Takao, "Gengo ni okeru ninshō no gainen ni tsuite" [On the concept of persons in language], *Keiōgijuku daigaku gengobunka kenkyūjo kiyō*, No. 2, 1971.

11. One interpretation of this problem can be found in Suzuki, Takao, "Torukogo no shinzoku yōgo ni kansuru ni-san no oboegaki" [Notes on kinship terms in Turkish], *Gengo kenkyū*, No. 51, 1967.

12. This term was first used in Bertrand Russell's *An Inquiry into Meaning and Truth* (Atlantic Heights, N.J., 1940).

13. Suzuki, Takao, "Torukogo no shinzoku yōgo in kansuru ni-san no oboegaki," *loc. cit.*

14. Suzuki, Takao, "On the Notion of Teknonymy," *Studies in Descriptive and Applied Linguistics*, *Bulletin of the Summer Institute in Linguistics*, Vol. 4 (Tokyo: International Christian University, 1967).

15. Schneider, David M. and Homans, George C., "Kinship Terminology and the American Kinship System," *American Anthropologist*, LVII (1955), pp. 1194–1208.

16. Goodenough, W. H., "Personal Names and Modes of Address," in Spiro, M. (ed.), *Context and Meaning in Cultural Anthropology* (New York and London, 1965).

17. Suzuki, Takao, "Shinzokumeishō ni yoru eigo no jikohyōgen to koshō," *loc. cit.*

18. Suzuki, Takao, "Gengo ni okeru ninshō no gainen ni tsuite," *loc. cit.*

19. Recently *otaku* has become increasingly more common as a term of address for non-relatives. It seems to be used especially when one does not have to place the addressee in terms of vertical (superior-inferior) human relations or when one needs a neutral pronoun.

20. Grootaers, W. A. and Shibata, Takeshi, *Goyaku* [Mistranslations] (Tokyo: Sanseido, 1967).

21. Takada, Makoto, "Can You Speak English?" *Gengo seikatsu*, No. 256, 1973.

22. The problem of fixation and non-diversification of roles, as well as that of self-designation dependent on the other, was originally discussed in Suzuki, Takao, "Nihonjin no gengo-ishiki to kōdō-yō [Linguistic consciousness and behavior patterns of the Japanese], *Shisō*, No. 572, 1972.

（新装版）英文版 ことばと文化
Words in Context

2001 年 8 月　第 1 刷発行
2006 年 8 月　第 2 刷発行

著　者　鈴木　孝夫

発行者　富田　充

発行所　講談社インターナショナル株式会社
　　　　〒 112-8652　東京都文京区音羽 1-17-14
　　　　電話　03-3944-6493（編集部）
　　　　　　　03-3944-6492（マーケティング部・業務部）
　　　　ホームページ　www.kodansha-intl.com

印刷・製本所　大日本印刷株式会社

JAPANESE SPIRITUALITY

HAGAKURE The Book of the Samurai   *Yamamoto Tsunetomo*   葉隠　山本常朝 著
Hagakure ("In the Shadow of Leaves") is a manual for the samurai classes consisting of a series of short anec-
dotes and reflections that give both insight and instruction in the philosophy and code of behavior that foster
the true spirit of Bushido—the Way of the Warrior. As featured in the film *Ghost Dog*.
Hardcover, 192 pages; ISBN 4-7700-2916-0   Paperback, 192 pages; ISBN 4-7700-1106-7

THE UNFETTERED MIND Writings of the Zen Master to the Sword Master
Soho Takuan   不動智神妙録　沢庵宗彭 著
Teachings of Zen master Takuan to Yagyū Munenori, who was awarded the post Miyamoto Musashi
coveted, of official sword teacher to the shoguns. Takuan's meditations on the sword in the essays pre-
sented here are classics of Zen thinking.
Hardcover , 144 pages; ISBN 4-7700-2947-0   Paperback, 104 pages; ISBN 0-87011-851-X

THE LIFE-GIVING SWORD Secret Teachings from the House of the Shogun
Yagyu Munenori   兵法家伝書　柳生宗矩 著
This is the new and definitive English translation of the classic text on the art of the No-Sword by seven-
teeth-century swordsman Yagyu Munenori. It is a treasury of proven Zen wisdom that will be of interest
to anyone in business or politics, as well as practitioners of the martial arts.
Hardcover; 192 pages; ISBN 4-7700-2955-5

BUSHIDO The Soul of Japan   *Inazo Nitobe*   武士道　新渡戸稲造 著
Written specifically for a Western audience in 1900 by Japan's under-secretary general to the League of
Nations, *Bushido* explains concepts such as honor and loyalty within traditional Japanese ethics. The book
is a classic, and as such throws a great deal of light on Japanese thinking and behavior, both past and present.
Hardcover , 160 pages; ISBN 4-7700-2731-1

THE BOOK OF FIVE RINGS   *Miyamoto Musashi*   五輪書　宮本武蔵 著
Setting down his thoughts on swordplay, on winning, and on spirituality, legendary swordsman Miyamoto
Musashi intended this modest work as a guide for his immediate disciples and future generations of
samurai. He had little idea he was penning a masterpiece that would be eagerly devoured by people in
all walks of life centuries after his death.
Hardcover, 160 pages; ISBN 4-7700-2801-6

MUSASHI An Epic Novel of the Samurai Era
Eiji Yoshikawa   宮本武蔵　吉川英治 著
This classic work tells of the legendary samurai who was the greatest swordsman of all time. "… a stir-
ring saga … one that will prove popular not only for readers interested in Japan but also for those who
simply want a rousing read."   —*The Washington Post*
Hardcover, 984 pages; ISBN 4-7700-1957-2

THE LONE SAMURAI The Life of Miyamoto Musashi
William Scott Wilson   宮本武蔵の肖像　ウィリアム・スコット・ウィルソン 著
The Lone Samurai is a landmark biography of Miyamoto Musashi, the legendary Japanese figure known
throughout the world as a master swordsman, spiritual seeker, and author of *The Book of Five Rings*.
Includes photographs, maps, glossary, and appendices.
Hardcover: 288 pages: ISBN 4-7700-2942-X

THE BOOK OF TEA   *Kakuzo Okakura*   茶の本　岡倉覚三 著
The seminal text on the meaning and practice of tea. Written 80 years ago, the book is less about tea than it
is about the philosophical and aesthetic traditions basic to Japanese culture.
Paperback, 168 pages; ISBN 4-7700-1542-9

KODANSHA INTERNATIONAL DICTIONARIES

Easy-to-use dictionaries designed for non-native learners of Japanese.

THE KODANSHA KANJI LEARNER'S DICTIONARY

新装版 漢英学習字典

The perfect kanji tool for beginners to advanced learners.
- Revolutionary SKIP lookup method
- Five lookup methods and three indices
- 2,230 entries and 41,000 meanings for 31,000 words

Paperback, 1060 pages (2-color); ISBN 4-7700-2855-5

KODANSHA'S ESSENTIAL KANJI DICTIONARY

新装版 常用漢英熟語辞典

A functional character dictionary that is both compact and comprehensive.
- Complete guide to the 1,945 essential *jōyō* kanji
- 20,000 common compounds
- Three indices for finding kanji

Paperback, 928 pages; ISBN 4-7700-2891-1

KODANSHA'S EFFECTIVE JAPANESE USAGE DICTIONARY

新装版 日本語使い分け辞典

A concise, bilingual dictionary that clarifies the usage of frequently confused words and phrases.
- Explanations of 708 synonymous terms
- Numerous example sentences

Paperback, 768 pages; ISBN 4-7700-2850-4

A DICTIONARY OF JAPANESE PARTICLES

てにをは辞典

Treats over 100 particles in alphabetical order, providing sample sentences for each meaning.
- Meets students' needs from beginning to advanced levels
- Treats principal particle meanings as well as variants

Paperback, 368 pages; ISBN 4-7700-2352-9

KODANSHA'S DICTIONARY OF BASIC JAPANESE IDIOMS

日本語イディオム辞典

All idioms are given in Japanese script and romanized text with English translations. There are approximately 880 entries, many of which have several senses.

Paperback, 672 pages; ISBN 4-7700-2797-4

A DICTIONARY OF BASIC JAPANESE SENTENCE PATTERNS

日本語基本文型辞典

Author of the best-selling *All About Particles* explains fifty of the most common, basic patterns and their variations, along with numerous contextual examples.
- Formulas delineating basic pattern structure
- Commentary on individual usages

Paperback, 320 pages; ISBN 4-7700-2608-0

www.kodansha-intl.com

JAPANESE LANGUAGE GUIDES

Easy-to-use guides to essential language skills

ALL ABOUT PARTICLES   新装版 助詞で変わるあなたの日本語   *Naoko Chino*

The most common and less common particles brought together and broken down into some 200 usages, with abundant sample sentences.

Paperback, 160 pages; ISBN 4-7700-2781-8

HOW TO TELL THE DIFFERENCE BETWEEN JAPANESE PARTICLES

Comparisons and Exercises   比べて分かる日本語の助詞   *Naoko Chino*

By grouping particles that are similar in function, this book helps students pin down differences in usage that would ordinarily take years to master. Definitions, sample sentences, usage notes, and quizzes enable students to move to a higher level of comprehension.

Paperback, 200 pages; ISBN 4-7700-2200-X

JAPANESE VERBS AT A GLANCE   新装版 日本語の動詞   *Naoko Chino*

Clear and straightforward explanations of Japanese verbs—their functions, forms, roles, and politeness levels.

Paperback, 180 pages; ISBN 4-7700-2765-6

JAPANESE SENTENCE PATTERNS FOR EFFECTIVE COMMUNICATION

A Self-Study Course and Reference   日本語文型ハンドブック   *Taeko Kamiya*

Presents 142 essential sentence patterns for daily conversation—all the ones an intermediate student should know, and all the ones a beginner should study to become minimally proficient in speaking. All in a handy, step-by-step format with pattern practice every few pages.

Paperback, 368 pages; ISBN 4-7700-2983-7

THE HANDBOOK OF JAPANESE VERBS   日本語動詞ハンドブック   *Taeko Kamiya*

An indispensable reference and guide to Japanese verbs aimed at beginning and intermediate students. Precisely the book that verb-challenged students have been looking for.

• Verbs are grouped, conjugated, and combined with auxiliaries
• Different forms are used in sentences   • Each form is followed by reinforcing examples and exercises

Paperback, 256 pages; ISBN 4-7700-2683-8

THE HANDBOOK OF JAPANESE ADJECTIVES AND ADVERBS

日本語形容詞・副詞ハンドブック   *Taeko Kamiya*

The ultimate reference manual for those seeking a deeper understanding of Japanese adjectives and adverbs and how they are used in sentences. Ideal, too, for those simply wishing to expand their vocabulary or speak livelier Japanese.

Paperback, 336 pages; ISBN 4-7700-2879-2

READ REAL JAPANESE: All You Need to Enjoy Eight Contemporary Writers

新装版 日本語で読もう   *Janet Ashby*

Original Japanese essays by Yoko Mori, Ryuichi Sakamoto, Machi Tawara, Shoichi Nejime, Momoko Sakura, Seiko Ito, Banana Yoshimoto, and Haruki Murakami. With vocabulary lists giving the English for Japanese words and phrases and also notes on grammar, nuance, and idiomatic usage.

Paperback, 168 pages; ISBN 4-7700-2936-5

JAPANESE LANGUAGE GUIDES

Easy-to-use guides to essential language skills

13 SECRETS FOR SPEAKING FLUENT JAPANESE

日本語をペラペラ話すための13の秘訣　*Giles Murray*

The most fun, rewarding, and universal techniques of successful learners of Japanese that anyone can put immediately to use. A unique and exciting alternative, full of lively commentaries, comical illustrations, and brain-teasing puzzles.

Paperback, 184 pages; ISBN 4-7700-2302-2

BREAKING INTO JAPANESE LITERATURE: Seven Modern Classics in Parallel Text

日本語を読むための七つの物語　*Giles Murray*

Read classics of modern Japanese fiction in the original with the aid of a built-in, customized dictionary, free MP3 sound files of professional Japanese narrators reading the stories, and literal English translations. Features Ryunosuke Akutagawa's "Rashomon" and other stories.

Paperback, 240 pages; ISBN 4-7700-2899-7

BREAKTHROUGH JAPANESE: 20 Mini Lessons for Better Conversation

日本語をネイティブのように話す秘訣　*Hitomi Hirayama*

A lively book that amplifies and reinforces the skills gained from more conventional textbooks. Designed to stimulate or rekindle a learner's curiosity, it is packed with activities that make language speaking fun. For all levels.

Paperback, 176 pages; ISBN 4-7700-2873-3

MAKING SENSE OF JAPANESE: What the Textbooks Don't Tell You

新装版 日本語の秘訣　*Jay Rubin*

"Brief, wittily written essays that gamely attempt to explain some of the more frustrating hurdles [of Japanese].... They can be read and enjoyed by students at any level." —*Asahi Evening News*

Paperback, 144 pages; ISBN 4-7700-2802-4

BEYOND POLITE JAPANESE: A Dictionary of Japanese Slang and Colloquialisms

新装版 役に立つ話しことば辞典　*Akihiko Yonekawa*

Expressions that all Japanese, but few foreigners, know and use every day. Sample sentences for every entry.

Paperback, 176 pages; ISBN 4- 7700-2773-7

LOVE, HATE and Everything in Between: Expressing Emotions in Japanese

新装版 日本語の感情表現集　*Mamiko Murakami*

Includes more than 400 phrases that are useful when talking about personal experience and nuances of feeling.

Paperback, 176 pages; ISBN 4-7700-2803-2

BASIC CONNECTIONS: Making Your Japanese Flow

新装版 日本語の基礎ルール　*Kakuko Shoji*

Explains how words and phrases dovetail, how clauses pair up with other clauses, how sentences come together to create harmonious paragraphs. The goal is to enable the student to speak both coherently and smoothly.

Paperback, 160 pages; ISBN 4-7700-2860-1

JAPANESE CORE WORDS AND PHRASES: Things You Can't Find in a Dictionary

新装版 辞書では解らない慣用表現　*Kakuko Shoji*

Some Japanese words and phrases, even though they lie at the core of the language, forever elude the student's grasp. This book brings these recalcitrants to bay.

Paperback, 144 pages; ISBN 4-7700-2774-5